7 Habits of
Happy People

The Hidden Secrets to Success

To my V ROSIe,

You are an incredible
Soul. Remember to shine
Your beautiful Light
Daily !!
With warmest wishes
Dr. Gold

Tanya Gold MD

ISBN: 978-0-578-77419-0

Dedication

To my Creator, my parents, sissy & Aunt Lorraine, and my beloved Stud Muffin.

To all those who believed in me and taught me to believe in myself.

To Chris who worked endless hours to help get this book marketed and finally get published.

A special note to my hubby, Drew, who told me to "write the damn thing already!"

Acknowledgment

There are many people I wish to thank. I want to acknowledge the editors and publishers for helping me to stay on track and complete this ultramarathon! A special shout out to Kimmie, who drew the beautiful illustrations. She remained patient and kind with me, through several revisions. Kathy, my coach, friend, organizer, editor, and key player, you really helped to turn this blob into a book. I couldn't have done it without you!

Thanks to my family and friends who kept asking when the book would come out. I realize that without them, this book would just be a great idea in my head where I jotted a few notes down. They gave me the encouragement to start and finish. Writing is a process— one I dreaded in grade school but feel it has improved with practice.

My aunt, Lorraine, and my sister, Marissa, who have endlessly read, rewritten, and reorganized everything I have sent them— thank you from the bottom of my heart. They're honest with their feedback (brutally honest at times), but encouraging, which I needed. I consider them my best friends. Thank you to the Power Gals (senior powerlifters), my coaches, patients, friends, yoga students, and extended family for giving me these stories to share. Whenever I felt like giving up, I would be reminded, "you're so close!" and through their love and enthusiasm, be encouraged to keep going. Thank you, mom and dad, for giving me life and teaching me to work hard, never give up, and do the right thing! Thank you, Hashem (G-d), for making me the determined and caring person I am.

They say it takes a village to raise a child, well, it's no different when writing a book. You need help!

I feel I've *given birth* to these pages, which come from the best in me. Drew… You're the love of my life, my best friend, and have been there through it all. You've seen my worst and still hung around. You were there when I was seriously thinking of throwing this whole book project down the toilet and egged me on, "so do it!" You know me so well that I don't easily accept defeat, and I like challenges. You supported me during the early mornings I got up to write and had to spend time away from you. I'm so blessed to have you in my life. To all those I told about the book, thank you for cheering me on.

Bella, Prince, my furry cherubs, thank you for your welcomed distraction. I know I spent many hours typing or recording what I wrote, but your loud woeful meows allowed me to take a break, so I could feed you (even though your food bowls were barely empty) and massage your fluffy bellies!

Now to my readers, I appreciate your support and look forward to meeting you one day if I haven't already. I also appreciate you sharing this precious gift of joy with others.

Caution

This book is about having FUN and enjoying life ….. & if you laugh too hard you may pee your pants. ☺ Please note this information does not constitute personal medical advice. If you have medical questions or plan to engage in any physical activity, please consult with your health care provider. One last thing, patient names have been changed for confidentiality.

Foreword

The pursuit of happiness is a common dream. Finding a simple means of achieving this is like winning the Lottery. Dr. Gold's L.A.U.G.H method is your golden ticket. She offers you a practical approach on how to cultivate joy from within. More than a book, this treasure of information allows you to take your life to the next level— making it even more meaningful and fulfilling.

Life can be hard, and no one will pretend to know or understand what you're going through, but despite the challenges, you can prevail. The compelling stories shared, including her own, attest to the indomitable will of the human spirit. They help you realize your own potential and that you are not alone. You are here for a reason and you deserve happiness!

Act Happy to Be Happy

There's no need to *wait* to feel good. The choice is yours! Dr. Gold realizes this is not easy, but she provides you with a simplified step by step approach to get you there. In a loving motherly fashion, she encourages you all along the way to do what you CAN and do your best. You learn that through action almost anything is possible, especially when you never give up. Like a muscle, joy grows with practice, one chuckle at a time. There is also scientific research to back it up. You can fake it, until you make it!

You may have grown up to believe you must be serious as an adult. Not true. The fun games and exercises invite you to become an active participant in the driver seat of your life directing your emotions to serve you. It's about transformation, giving yourself permission "to let the kid inside come out and play." You get to decide each moment how you want to feel and personalize your journey to lead an optimal life. This book is your map.

Each precious habit you adopt can help you become more lighthearted, boosting your health, and further strengthening your resiliency to heart-ache and diseases. There is suffering in this world, no doubt, but the antidote is not to suffer more, it's to sprinkle in cheer. As we brighten this world, starting with ourselves, we get closer to world peace, because it's hard to hurt someone you love. In addition, we recognize we are all interconnected. Laughter is a conduit in this web, that's why it's so contagious and feels marvelous. It's a necessary ingredient to lead a balanced life and find your bliss. Growing up in a small village in India, I often laughed at the "small things." After becoming a physician, and moving to a big glitzy city, I became stressed and noticed that I rarely enjoyed anything. Consequently, I found myself feeling sad, isolated and alone, even among all these people. This book reminded me how I transformed myself by applying more laughter in my life. It's a free pass to unleash the child within and recognize that you don't require a reason to smile and giggle. You can do it to feel better.

This book is an essential guide, meant to be shared and experienced. It's your license to a fruitful life that can continue to blossom and get sweeter with time. I hope this book uplifts you, like it did for me!

Keep laughing! Ha, ha! Dr. Kataria ☺

Founder of Laughter Yoga

My Story

It wasn't supposed to turn out this way. I had it all planned out. Married at 25, kids at 30, successful job at 35, retire early after I make millions of dollars and become quite famous, and live happily ever after. Well... it didn't quite work out that way. How about this, instead:

1. I got married at 30 (no worries just five years past my plan)

2. I am almost 50 and still no kids... hmmm (I figure I can still adopt or continue to borrow them from my big family!)

3. Working long hours in medical school, residency, and in a traditional medical practice— I got burned out.

4. I became very sick in my 20's and 30's with Lyme's disease, severe arthritis, and uveitis (a severe eye condition that could lead to blindness). Bummer, definitely not in my game plan— is it ever?

5. I lost several jobs (which kinda sucked too) and was told "you can't be sick! You're a doctor." Agree, now tell that to the man upstairs.

6. Far from my millions, fame, and retirement, I was almost bankrupt in my 40's. Not really the Cinderella story I was looking for. "Life doesn't always work out the way you want." Most of the time, it doesn't. So, whaddya going to do, give up, roll over and play dead or get up and fight?

This book is about reclaiming back your life. Even in the darkest of circumstances, there is a flicker of hope. You can learn effective ways to bring more joy into your life— live more passionately and get excited. This is not a fantasy as we will model real people who are doing it— learning their habits and practicing with fun games and exercises.

This book is a roadmap, not leading you to a fairy tale, but helping you find your optimal life. It varies for each person. That's why it's so important to not just gloss through the activities, but take them seriously and DO them!!

This book is not for the faint of heart. It's for those willing to make real changes in their lives— willing to DO things to make their lives better. I won't say it'll be easy, but it will be well worth it!

Turning a corner

Even in the darkest of circumstances, there is light... and hope. That's what Gaby Giffords found. Sometimes you just gotta roll with the punches (or the shots!). This Arizona congresswoman's life changed drastically after she became target practice for a madman. He shot her in the head along with 18 others at a peaceful rally 'for the people.' Miraculously she lived! Surprisingly, despite all that Gaby's been through, she's not bitter. Even with a speech impediment and a troubling gait, among other things, she feels blessed to still be alive. No one could blame her for being angry, but according to her husband, in her book, 'Gaby,' she still manages to jump out of bed excited and ready to make this world a better place. She focuses on her mission.

Visualize Your Optimal Life

Stand up or sit up straight (if possible)

Take at least 3 deep breaths & Smile

Visualize Your DREAM Life (What are you passionate about? What inspires you? What are you doing? Where are you? Who are you with? Are you travelling? Be there. See what you see. Hear what you hear. Feel it. Notice any scents. Don't hold back and know that almost anything is possible!)

Now jot down or record what you saw. Why is this important to you?

(Are you doing it now, or just reading on? Stop now and do this, if you want to kick-start the changes you wish to see in your life.)

"I'm still here, and I've got much work to do." Her strength, enthusiasm, and courage inspire me to value what's truly important in my life: G-d, my wonderful husband, my family & friends, my patients, my yoga students, and yes, my adorable kitties (they are my babies!). What's important in _your_ life? Are you living your life to its fullest?

You must know what you want so you can get there. Unless what are you aiming for? It's like trying to book a flight, unsure of your destination. Pick something. You can always change it later. For myself, my passion is getting people WELL long term (living strong, happy, vibrant lives). It's an honor to serve them. However, I realize I can't do that if I don't take care of myself.

As you can imagine, when my fairy tale life did not turn out as planned (far from it), I became disillusioned. I got frustrated, angry and sad. What do I do now? I felt lost and confused. The stress added up and then I got sick. Very sick — diagnosed with uveitis, which threatened my vision (making it blurry). It turned my eye beet red and made it feel as if a dagger was poking through— burning and throbbing as if I had a black eye. I became so sensitive to light. I had to wear sunglasses, even indoors. Some classmates poked fun at me, asking me why I was trying to act cool.

Years later, I suffered from severe arthritis in my neck. My doctors wanted to operate. I didn't. I knew there had to be a different way. My doctors did their best, but the pain meds they prescribed left me drowsy and made it difficult to concentrate and work. I also gained enormous amounts of weight from the steroids, to the point my patients were congratulating me. "So how far along are you?"

After my pants tore, I knew that something had to change: ME.

Centering on being miserable was not fun. I had enough. With so much practice, I was getting good at feeling lousy.

I'M DONE!

As the Bible states, "You are what you think" (Proverbs 23:7). In other words, "where focus goes, energy flows!" (Tony Robbins). One wise yogi stated, "When you *worry,* you pray for what you *don't* want." I didn't want to be sad anymore, yet I didn't know HOW to get happy, how to bring more joy into my life when I felt so bad.

Then I remembered Norman Cousins, author of "Anatomy of an Illness" who relieved his excruciatingly painful symptoms of ankylosing spondylitis with laughter and vitamin C.

Laugher? How interesting! It was worth a shot. I had nothing to lose and much to gain. I didn't want to cry anymore. I wanted to laugh.

Besides funny movies (which Norman Cousins used in order to stimulate his laughter), I wanted to explore other options to make me happy as I couldn't always say "hey boss I am taking a 2-hour break to watch this movie." I realize now that no one can *make* you happy. This is something you do for yourself. What are you going to do when you don't know something? Google it, of course! I looked up simple ways to cackle and came across Laughter Yoga. I even found you could chuckle with others on the phone in something called "The Laugher Hotline."

Who ya gonna call?

No, not ghostbusters! The Laughter Hotline is a free call that anyone can dial into to laugh with others. They also have a skype version (skype laughter club). No joke. I was shy to call, at first, because I thought my laugh wasn't good enough and embarrassed because I snort (yes, I had low self—esteem issues too), I finally just called in. I found the laughter infectious, and it became genuine after a period of time. Once I giggled (even on command), I began to feel a release; a lightness take over me. With just one session under my belt, I felt noticeably better. No pain meds thus far provided me with such relief both mentally and physically. It relaxed my neck and the rest of my body and brought in hope. Towards the end of the call, the leader had us take a few deep breaths and then asked us to share what we were grateful for. As I rehearse this fun exercise almost daily, it's easy to turn on. Just as lifting weights strengthens muscles, so do our laughter muscles build cheer within us, giggle by giggle.

Receiving so much benefit, I knew I wanted to share this incredible gift with others. That's why I became certified in Laughter Yoga and a laughter leader through The World Laughter Tour (seriously, you can look it up laughteryoga.org and worldlaughtertour.com).

The Gift

Now, over ten years later, I am happy to say, NO PAIN and NO SURGERY. My bouts of uveitis have also diminished. I am blessed, and it may sound strange to say this, but I am glad it happened. It taught me to appreciate my health and not take it for granted; because I did. Prior to this, I had good health, would rarely fall ill (even with a cold), and I never missed a day of school (not even in medical school).

But I realize all this is NOT just luck. I work hard at taking care of myself and staying the course of managing my thoughts. I now work for myself, having become the proud owner of a growing integrative medical practice, "Dr. Gold's Optimal Living Institute." I get to spend time with my patients, providing them with compassionate care, listening to their concerns, and working earnestly to get them well long term. I can empathize, having been quite sad and sick myself.

Many new people I meet are surprised to learn that I used to be this way (because now I'm usually chipper and have often received the nickname "Dr. Smiley and Dr. Sunshine.")

"You mean you're NOT naturally jolly?" they ask. No. Far from it. I was not born with a sunny disposition. Until I found laughter, I was quite cynical and looked for the worst-case scenario.

These thoughts resonated with me when I was on a beautiful beach with my nephew at sunset. The sky glowed. Nice breeze, as the warm sea enveloped our bodies. The serene blue waves lapped the seashore in a flawless sequence. Everything appeared perfect, yet my nephew continued to harp on the small seaweed he found "quite gross" floating in the water. I finally told him to look up. Once he did, his face lit up like it was Christmas. The bright sun, amidst a dazzling array of colors, had us mesmerized. This new perspective changed his outlook, just as addressing my illnesses with laughter had changed mine.

Like my nephew, I needed to remind myself to "Look Up" and recognize who I am. My true self wants to be happy. That imposter who brings me down (for long periods) is not me. It's some sort of a virus in thinking I received way back when. It may have served a purpose, like an IBM mainframe computer from the 1950s— what was perhaps useful then is now obsolete. But unless we examine what no longer serves us, we can get stuck.

Today, I smile and laugh often, so I CAN feel joy, and it does come much easier now. My hope is the same for you… that by reading this book, you will learn effective tools to put into practice and gain momentum to lead a happy and fulfilling life.

Contents

Page Left Blank Intentionally

Introduction

Mom is with me

After a parent leaves or falls ill, you tend to have to grow up a little quicker. That's what I did after my mom completed her life early. As the eldest, I was protective of my little sister and felt as if I took mom's place. Understandably, I was mad and, of course, sad that she left. I thought I did something wrong for G-d to take her away so soon.

Now I realize my mom is with me, and I can take her wherever I go. I feel her presence guiding me. She was a phenomenal writer, and when the words I write flow easily, I know they come from her. Giving me life and a lifetime of love, I'm forever thankful. This book is as much hers as it is mine.

Once I found more laughter in my life, I realized I could let go of all the pain I felt. I could be cheerful, calm, and happy. I could feel joy at knowing I'm doing the best I can, and that is enough. I see my mom's beautiful smile and know I will be ok (*and so will you*, if you are going through a rough time). I can let go of being serious all the time (Lighten UP!)

and have fun! Working on this book gave me a renewed sense of purpose. It has profoundly changed my perspective on living, which I can now pass on to YOU (my readers) and to my patients, helping them to see things with a wide optimistic lens, especially if they're struggling. For example, one of my patients Ken is going through a bitter divorce. His wife used to beat him. Instead of blaming himself, Ken is realizing "he's a catch" and deserving of deep love and respect. He's also FREE and has become more bright-eyed as he has begun to laugh and smile more, focusing on all of his attributes.

This is More Than Just A Book

I believe fun comes when you decide to have it. This book will show you how to laugh during challenges. In addition to the fun games, there are also YouTube videos I created on my channel, 'drgoldfunyoga.' Let your inner child come out and play! I realize it can feel weird to laugh on purpose and may not be part of cultural expectations. You may have been taught to take life seriously. However, now is the time to give yourself permission to smile and have a good time. You can engage in these exercises at work and with the kids.

Basically, almost anywhere you are, laughter can come to you, bringing more JOY into your world

Let's Get Started

Getting in the mood starts with connecting your mind with your body. Let's begin with some mindful breathing.

Breathe Mindfully

1. Sit up tall with shoulders back and down.

2. Smile. Take three deep breaths IN and OUT (more if you need them). Think of something wonderful in your life. Yes, there is something!

3. What are you grateful for? For me, I am blessed that you are here, reading this. Even if we have not yet met, I feel like we are kindred spirits.

4. Inhale for 4 seconds, allowing the belly to fully inflate, like a balloon.

5. Pause for 4 seconds.

6. Exhale slowly for 8 seconds to empty all the air out as the abdomen contracts.

7. Pause for another 4 seconds. Repeat 3X or more until you feel relaxed.

Smile

Smiling is a universal welcome. It is the gateway to laughter. As humans, all of us share this connection, even with complete strangers. If you are not used to smiling, let's practice. Smiling 101 is something I did with one of my patients, who told me he hadn't laughed in a long time. Once we got going, he couldn't stop! 😊

Don't worry if you haven't done this in a while, it will come back to you, like riding a bike. Start massaging one side of your cheek and raise it up, show some teeth or gum or whatever you got. *I once asked my patient to show me her teeth and she took them out!*

Some people are embarrassed to smile because their teeth are rotten, or they don't have any. My sister didn't want to smile because of her braces. Whatever the case, know you should never deprive yourself of one of the greatest gifts because of what others may think! Those *who matter* won't care, and those who care *don't matter!* Of course, if you need to see a dentist, please do.

The Smile Game

(see dgoli.com "FUN Games" with Dr. Gold)

1. Genuinely smile at 3 people.

2. Feel free to add a greeting i.e. Good Morning, Hey, What's up! Hello, How are you? Buenos Dias, Ciao, Shalom, Howdy partner, Top of the morning to ya.

3. Continue to smile at more people (count how many) and see if you can beat your score.

4. How does it feel to smile? How does it feel when someone smiles back? If you are not used to smiling, I promise it can get easier with practice.

Do this wherever you are— at the grocery store, the mall, at family gatherings, running errands, or at work. It will definitely be challenging with a mask on, but you can tell by the creases in their eyes.

** Caution: Smiling or laughing can be city or area dependent. I grew up in NYC in the 1980s and smiling or saying hello to the wrong person could get you beat up. In fact, I was taught to deliberately not look at people on the street, let alone converse with them. Depending on the person, they may ask, "What are you lookin' at?" When my family moved to Charlotte, NC, and a stranger gave me a friendly hello, I just stared at him. My dad nudged me and told me, *"it's ok to smile and say hello back,* we're in the south now. *"*

Smiling helps you get ready for happiness. Getting started is half the battle (overcoming the head-trash that keeps us stagnant.) So, let's address this.

How to Overcome

Many folks are not happy in this world. According to the World Health Organization (WHO), 350 million people worldwide, including children, suffer from depression[1]. Sixteen million of those individuals come from the US. This

---

[1]Marcus, Marina, M. Taghi Yasamy, Mark van van Ommeren, Dan Chisholm, and Shekhar Saxena. 2012. "Depression: A Global Public Health Concern: (517532013004)."https://www.who.int/mental_health/management/depression/who_paper_depression_wfmh_2012.pdf

does not include those that are too ashamed to even get evaluated. Forty million Americans also suffer from anxiety. Society has reason to feel this way with natural disasters, terror, and cruelty happening daily in the world. Just turn on the news, and you will see. But amid darkness and despair, as Martin Luther King reminds us, we may just need to turn on the light. How do we do this? We can do it daily by making room for compassion, love, kindness, and joy in our hearts. It's through these positive attributes— followed by courage, faith, and hope that our great leaders have been able to overcome all the odds. The teachings of Gandhi, Mother Theresa, Nelson Mandela, Martin Luther King, JFK, Jesus, and Muhammad, are just a few examples (don't worry we'll give you some pointers in the chapters to follow).

Who in your life has helped you become the person you are today— either by showing you the way or by becoming a warning of what you did not want to become? The truth is that happiness must be cultivated and practiced. It's easy to be happy when everything is going well, but how often does that happen? Real-life doesn't work that way. Bumps in the road pop up, especially the longer you live. When you learn how to allow joy to be your foundation, happiness becomes a result in your life more and more. If you have been sad, I can relate. I, too, have lived many years in despair. I have felt hopeless and overwhelmed, a confession that surprises many of my current friends because they usually find me smiling. But for a long time, my cup seemed half-empty. When I compared myself to others, I was jealous of those who seemed to have everything going well for them, while my boat seemed like it was sinking. Have you ever faced a time when you said: "I can't take it anymore"? Well, that came for me the morning my pants tore because I had gained so much weight.

My doctors placed me on high dose steroids, which had me eating more than my husband. I ended up wearing his pants that day because that's all I could fit into. Later, a patient congratulated me and asked me how far along I was. Not pregnant, but extremely embarrassed, I went for a walk with tears streaming down my face. I was searching for answers. I prayed to G-d, asking for a response. I knew there had to be a natural way to improve the searing pain running through my neck and arm that would wake me up in the middle of the night, screaming. As I wandered around, I found my way into Shapes, a women's gym that had a pool and indoor jacuzzi. I signed up on the spot. There I found I could exercise in the pool without pain. I was experiencing severe neck arthritis in my 30s, and this subjected me to narcotics. My doctors wanted to operate. I didn't. Having witnessed similar patients, still suffering who became disabled and hooked on opioids even after surgery, I didn't want to become another statistic. I needed to figure this out. My goal was to improve naturally, even though I knew no one who had done this before, and I decided to tread my own path. As I alluded to earlier, laughter played a pivotal role in my recovery. It helped me change my perspective and focus on what was going WELL in my life.

Planning for the future— specifically by creating my roadmap of opening my own integrative medical practice D'Goli— helped me heal. Hence, the reason for this book so that I could share my story and instill hope. That's why the first Habit will focus on Purpose. What is yours?

Happiness comes easy for some, NOT for me. I am the kind of person who needs to work at it. *It does get easier with practice.*

Growing up shy, quiet, and serious, I could be in a room and go unnoticed. Laughing with strangers was the furthest thing from my mind. Fortunately, the laughter hotline had a prerecording, which I started with because I was too embarrassed to call into the live line. It felt weird at first, but as I heard others laugh, I began to feel the heaviness in my body lift. Soon, I felt comfortable joining in.

After several months of doing this, and feeling much better, I suddenly couldn't get the automated line to work, so I finally gathered enough courage to call in live. No big deal once I did. It's amazing how BIG things can seem in your head. Mark Twain comments, "I have had a lot of worries in my life, most of which never happened!"

Choosing Joy

At any moment, one can choose how they want to feel. Viktor Frankl, a psychiatrist, realized this. That's how he was still able to chuckle while in the concentration camp. He was stripped of everything, but they couldn't take away his humanness. That's also how he retained his sanity. His purpose was to finish his book, which he did after the war. He titled it *"Man's Search for Meaning."* He realized those that had survived the atrocities had a compelling reason to do so. These included motivation to find a loved one, complete a passion, or tell others the horror of the Holocaust so it would 'never again' happen. He had to rewrite his entire book, as the earlier manuscript was confiscated by the Nazis before he could publish it.

Consider this…"What makes you come alive?"

(Take 5 minutes to answer this important question.)

I am asking you to find the answer to this question because what we need in this world are people who are alive, according to Howard Thurman, civil rights leader, and author.

Let's delve into the 7 Habits of Extremely Happy People now.

There's more to happiness than what we can see. Much of it lies below the surface.

Habit #1— Live with Purpose

"The tragedy of life is Not Death, BUT what we let DIE inside of us while we LIVE."

-Norman Cousins

All my dad ever wanted for his kids was for them to be happy. "Tanya, live without regrets. Live your dream life NOW, and don't ever wonder what if!" He led by example, running his own successful accounting firm for over 40 years and becoming a father to many, fulfilling his lifelong dreams.

"It's a lot more rewarding to tell someone how you did it, rather than harbor disappointment over not even trying."

What is YOUR purpose?

Base your answer not on what somebody else wants for you, but on what YOU want for yourself? Take the time to think about it.

What are you passionate about?

What are you willing to wake up early or go to bed late for?

These answers won't come easy, so I'll advise you to take a few minutes to think about it and write down whatever comes to mind. Don't hold back and be honest with yourself. Use the earlier visualization exercise to help. It's fine if they overlap.

There are some caveats — try to be more specific. If you write such general things as 'Save the World' or 'Be Happy'— stop right there and think again. How specifically do you plan to be happy, and how specifically do you think you can save the world?

For example, you may want to set up a scholarship fund for ten well-deserving college students (or even 1) who may not be able to afford it otherwise. Once you have a plan in mind, you can find out ways to make things happen. For instance, in the example mentioned here, you can use other people's money (donations) or learn how to acquire residual income and earn more while you sleep! There is money out there, the question is, is it getting funneled to you? Getting what you need can help make your dreams come true. I'm not going to say it's easy, because it's not. It will take a lot of hard work, discipline, and commitment on your part; but, aren't you worth it? Living up to your potential and living a wholesome life is a lot more fun than watching it from the sidelines. It's like playing an engaging game; you'll grow as a person and enjoy it more if you participate.

The root word of 'purpose' comes from an old French word from the 12th century 'porpos' which means 'to aim or your intention.' So, the purpose is the reason for which something is done. I define purpose as something that excites you and doesn't feel like work. It is something you are willing to jump out of bed for at 4 am and continue doing it for hours. It is something that makes time fly. Helping people is my passion, specifically getting them well and teaching them effective methods to feel happier. Hence the reason for this book and yes, I have been getting up early to do this, since I am still working full time while writing this (it was 1:51 a.m. when I wrote this piece).

So why do folks NOT accomplish their dreams?

1. They may think it's not possible, it's foolish or it's too late. They may also be afraid— scared of failure or success.

2. They blame others for their inactions.

3. They may not know what their purpose is.

4. They may get caught up in what others want for them (and never really think about what they want for themselves). If you don't dictate your life, someone else will!

Number four was me. When I was 5, my dad told me I would be a doctor. I had no idea what he was talking about. I just looked at him, confused. I didn't contemplate much else. For a split second, I thought of becoming a baton twirler, but dad knocked that down pretty quickly. "Tanya, do you really want to be on the sidelines cheering for others, or do you want others to be the ones cheering for you?"

I thought about it. And who doesn't want applause? He had a point. This was the time before "Bring it on"— there were no cheering squads that competed (that I knew about). You rooted for the football team, but I did like the cute cheerleading outfits. So, when people asked me what I wanted to be, before I had a chance to answer, my dad told them: "This is my doctor." It sounded good, and they looked impressed. I realized after a few years in practice that mainstream medicine was not for me.

My advisor from my family medicine residency at UTMB and mentor Vic Sierpina, MD (also a certified acupuncturist), predicted this would happen. "Tanya, don't do it, you'll never fit in." He was right.

I liked spending time with my patients and treating the root cause of their ailments, which is challenging in a busy practice that stresses treating symptoms rather than the whole person. As was the culture, many people *waited* to get sick before they came in and then wanted an immediate fix. I wondered if we offered more prevention, would they have staved off more of these illnesses.

Fortunately, I took the time to think of what I wanted and opened my own holistic medical practice, so I could get patients well long-term and be my own boss.

Do you have reasons or results?

Are you living your purpose— that is, your dream goal? If you are working towards it, good for you, but if you're getting stuck and not making progress, get help. This book will guide you. If you do not have a deadline for completion, make one. A dream without a timeline is just that. For those who are not living their dreams, all of us have a story for

WHY it's not getting done. I'm too old, too young, not enough money, too busy, no time, not smart enough, I have no idea what I want, etc.

Let me share another story about guts and determination.

"There's always a way if you want something bad enough."

These are a few words of advice from my 99-year-old powerlifter friend (and mentor), Ms. Edith Traina.

The entire idea is to "never give up. You never fail if you never quit, and you'll never know if you never try. Just keep hangin' in there, show up and do what you can."

Edith admits it takes her a while to get goin' in the morning, and many times, it feels easier to just roll over in bed. She doesn't give in, however. She gets her butt up because she knows it's good for her. She's never regretted a workout and feels so much better afterward.

Edith is a prime example of getting knocked down. With five kids, her husband got polio and had to be placed in an iron lung at only 34. An iron lung looks like a large round coffin, except the patient's head, sticks out. It works by blowing air into the patient's lung via intubation tubes, using a positive pressure ventilator. You're immobilized in that thing and can't go anywhere. Basically, the tube breathes for you; it had to as Edith's husband was paralyzed. This happened in the 1950s when most women stayed home, raised the children, and didn't work. She told me as a woman, she couldn't even get a loan at the bank without her husband's signature. Those were the rules. With so many kids, she got three jobs in order to make ends meet. Otherwise, she would be reliant on the government for assistance.

President Franklin D. Roosevelt backed welfare, a federal aid program, to the poor— which came about for the 1st time in American history in 1935. She decided she would "have none of that" and instead be self-reliant and make it work. She lived in the Bronx and worked in the garment district. She smoked and took "No Doze" to deal with the stress and stay awake. When she slept, she has "no idea. I had no time to be tired!" Often if you just keep showing up and continue to try with good intention and patience, good things can come of it. Edith reminds me to learn from my slip-ups and keep going. "I keep making mistakes all the time," Edith states with her charismatic grin (and a little dimple showing), "and G-d hasn't struck me down yet. In fact, I think he's there to catch me." Do you want to wallow in self-pity, or do you want to win? The simple fact is you win when you're living your purpose.

What do you know?

I was still a kid when I entered college. I had just turned 17 after I skipped a grade. But how are you supposed to know what you want to do with the rest of your life when you are so young? People tell you, you have so much time, but then there is this pressure to choose a major if you want to graduate in four years. Especially as a pre-med student, there are several core classes you need. So, what do you do? You succumb to the pressure or spend extra time in school, figuring it out. Either way, you've got to know that you're not stuck. Even if you choose a major, you end up not liking or the career choices you choose, you don't find appealing anymore, know that you can change that too.

At the end of the day, it is YOUR LIFE.

So, again, what do you want to do with it?

What is the purpose of your life?

I admit I liked college life so much I could see myself staying and considered becoming a perpetual student, but I thought of all the student loans I would accrue and doubt my dad would be too keen on this as he was also helping pay the bills.

There are so many professions out there, how do you know which one to choose? It can be scary in the real world.

That's why it's a good idea to sit down and think it over and figure out your life's mission (knowing you can alter it anytime, but do try to stick to something, so you really give it a shot).

So, apart from the confusion and demands of life, there are many other reasons why people don't follow through on what excites them. Let's explore them now.

Reason 1— It's NOT POSSIBLE

"Whether you think you can, or you think you can't, you're right."

-Henry Ford

Like the mom in Hairspray pointed out, "I wanted to own a coin-operated laundromat, but I quickly came down from that cloud in the sky."

We grow up. We may have been told, 'There's no way you can do that' 'You're just not that smart' or 'You don't have enough money' or 'You don't have the know-how, or the will power' or 'It's just not for you' or 'You are not good enough!'

The list goes on.

So, you accept what others tell you, and you don't even try.

My pre-med advisor in college told me not to even bother applying to medical school: "You will never get in."

"Watch me," I told him boldly!

"What happens if you don't even apply?" my dad asked. He was right... that's a 100% guarantee that you will never get in!

Sadly, the same advisor told many of my classmates (whose life-long dream was to become a doctor) the same thing. Several listened to him and never even bothered taking the MCATs (a required test for admissions). I know he was just doing what he thought was right. They, like me, probably didn't have stellar test scores or grades, and there's only a finite number of people that get accepted each year compared to those who apply.

My advisor was right. The first time I applied, I didn't get in. But I didn't give up. I worked harder, reapplied (took a year off), and finally got in. One thing my advisor didn't know about me is my GRIT. I don't give up easily. Grit is the ability to persevere despite obstacles. Life is full of them, and it's the one who sees IMPOSSIBLE as "I'M POSSIBLE" that makes things happen.

You probably know people like this who seem to move mountains. How the heck did they pull that off and with no resources and no money? I heard a story of a Nigerian man who wanted to go to a learning seminar so bad that he panhandled in the streets of New York City. He simply asked, "May I get $1" (he didn't even tell people why). After 2 hours, he had enough money.

When you have a strong enough WHY, you will find a way. That's why it is so important to know your purpose or at least come up with something that serves others— of course, in a healthy matter.

You at least have a shot if you try. If you never try, the answer is always NO. That's always stuck with me. If it's your dream, you are the only one who can make it happen.

Let me share a story about one of my favorite films coming to fruition. There once was a person who wrote a movie script. It was good, and he knew it, he just needed to sell it to a producer. He had three conditions— he owned the rights, he got to produce it the way he wanted, and he wanted to star in it because he knew this would amount to something great if he could get his important message across. Now, this man was not famous, and he had a chiseled face. What really stuck out was that he talked 'a little funny,' which turned out to be a deal-breaker for many studios.

He was broke and was living out of his car. He even had to sell his best friend, his bullmastiff "Butkus" (his precious dog) to survive. With about $100 in the bank, one producer offered to buy all the rights for $300K. He told him he would find somebody else to star in it. He turned him down. Can you believe it? I don't think I would, under those circumstances. But this gutsy guy, like his character, wouldn't quit. He had a purpose, and he had heart. That's probably why I love this movie so much because it teaches you anything is possible. He finally found someone willing to produce this epic film agreeing to all of his terms. Do you know who it is? You might have heard of Sylvester Stallone, who played Rocky (and the many sequels of the movie). And now Creed is a continuation of the story about the next generation, all because one guy wouldn't quit.

Think of all the generations who have benefited from these movies. I know I have. It's kept me tough when I wanted to give up. I still play the song by Survivor "Eye of the Tiger" at times when I am training or writing, which motivates me to keep going.

Remember when you quit, you are not only letting yourself down but all those who could benefit from YOU! Don't be selfish. Share your gifts. All of us have them! ☺

Reason 2— "It's not my fault."

A guy I dated while in medical school (I'll call him Noah), blamed many of his failures on his parent's divorce. Mind you; this was over ten years ago. He said that their divorce was the reason why he had trouble with commitment and would probably never know his kids well (because he would have the same fate as his parents— a failed marriage).

He told me this by our second date. He was like George from Seinfeld (pro at predicting the worst-case scenario). Noah was working on his Ph.D. in psychology and said he would probably never finish. Everyone was riding him. Again, his parents never taught him 'good coping skills.'

"How's that working out for you?" I finally said to him. I'd had enough of his excuses and wanted him to get past this. When are you going to grow up and realize YOU are an adult? You are responsible for your decisions now, not your parents.

Is it your parent's fault if you don't complete your assignment or act like a jackass? As you can imagine, this didn't go over too well.

That's why we broke up. He was a sweet guy but would self-sabotage many things, including our relationship— yes, by acting up, and the chemistry just wasn't there.

We worked great as friends, and that made it easier for me to call him on his BS (faulty Belief Systems).

As friends, Noah didn't mind me pushing his buttons, because he knew I cared. He knew if he didn't shape up, he wasn't going to graduate. Thankfully, he did. He let go of the blame and got to work. Noah also completed his book and now has a wonderful family. He's now in the driver's seat of his own life (not his parents)! But what if you don't know what you want to do.

Reason 3— Unsure of Your Purpose

You are not here to just take up space or use up oxygen. You exist for a reason. Your life matters!

Some people don't know their purpose in life. Don't feel bad; I wasn't sure what mine was for a long time, and even now, I realize it is evolving and can change.

What do you want people to say about your life? What do you want to be remembered as doing?

Create Your Road Map

You need a roadmap for your journey. Otherwise, you can get lost. Don't worry, I will give you the tools to create one.

In Psychology Today, a study showed that people can't always recognize what's good for them— what brings them joy. You may have wanted to put the word '*happy*' there, but let me tell you why you should go for *'joy'* instead.

Happiness is short-lived and material based. It is dependent on something outside of you, meaning that it is conditional. You realize this when you think, "I will be happy when…so and so happens." And then complete it with "…when I make my 1st million" or "…when I graduate" or "…when I have my baby" or "…when I find true love."

One way to understand the difference is this.

Joy is long-lasting, unconditional as it comes from within. It's not dependent on something happening to you or you buying some material possessions or someone liking you or praising you for something you have done. It's genuine, memorable, and comes from your heart like the love for your children or volunteering for a cause you believe in. You do it because it's the right thing to do, not thinking about what you'll get out of it or what other people will think.

As many people use the term happy instead of joy, I will continue that trend and use these words interchangeably, but now you understand the distinctions.

Think about this: if you can't find joy (or happiness) now, how likely are you to find it later? If your happiness is external, you will always be searching for it, and it may never seem enough. Joy begins when you decide to experience it and let in 'self-love.' Then you can open up to so many more possibilities in life, including following your heart's passion.

Happiness is I have a luxurious home.

Joy is spending quality time with YOU and the people you love in that home!

I've met people who do not understand the difference between joy and happiness, so they go chasing after the wrong thing. This is one of the reasons why we have depressed and anxious people in this world and those unsure of their true purpose. I suspect if they did know what made them happy, they would be doing it by now. We do what we know. What you don't know can hurt you— like not realizing how to obtain good health, wealth, or fulfillment.

So, getting back to figuring out your purpose, find your JOY. Allow it to be something that is serving and healthy.

Michael loved his car

That was an understatement. He worshipped it. He shined, buffed, and waxed it weekly, all by himself (as no one could do as good a job as he). He admired it daily and barely drove it. It was a red 1964 Corvette. That baby made him grin from ear to ear, and it was his pride and joy. After his daughter (interestingly named Joy) got sick, he realized he spent more time with this damn machine than he did with his own child. Now, this was an inanimate object that couldn't speak to him or love him. Brittany (he named the car) couldn't hug or kiss him. Finally, he broke up with Brittany, and he began catching up on lost time with his precious little angel, Joy.

His love grew as he got to know Joy all over again. She recovered, thankfully, and they played soccer together on the weekends. He got to take her to college and watch her (which seemed to happen almost overnight) become an accomplished attorney, and a loving mother and wife.

The great part is that there are people who've been through similar situations to you and prevailed. If you're struggling to find your purpose or challenged to reach it, get help, and ask, what can I learn from others?

Believe

Meet Marva, a kindhearted soul diagnosed with MS. Her condition was progressing, and her neurologist told her to prepare for the worse— wheelchair and extreme pain and maybe a few more years at best to live. She refused to accept this grim prognosis. Ten years later, she's still walking, with some minor discomfort, but it is manageable. Understand that healing can come from within, and it comes with a strong belief that you can improve.

So, if you have an illness — know that it **does not define you** — and you can make progress, getting stronger and healthier. In the meantime, decide on your purpose and start making it happen! Life is too short not to.

Do you know anyone like this?

Rick is a sweet guy in his 40's but looks more like 60. He reeks of tobacco and calls me 'Mama.' Rick tells me that he is in constant pain and will *never* get better. He lives on Oxycontin and Xanax, which provide some relief. It's interesting; I find the folks who believe they'll never improve usually don't. And the ones (even with similar conditions) who tell me with conviction that they will overcome, seem to find a way (remember Henry Ford's quote— whether you think you can or think you can't, you're right).

See, if you are not looking for answers, your brain will not find them.

As you've heard, what you focus on expands. If you live in fear, you become fearful. Just check out how people respond to the news. Our brain is designed to keep us alive, NOT to make us happy. With that knowledge, we can train ourselves for joy, and that's where laughter comes in. Instead of months of therapy (which I feel is still important), laughter can provide you with joy today— no need to wait. Still, undergo treatment (if you need it) but complement it with G-d's gift.

Laughter is our natural way to instant relief. Because when you are heartily laughing, you are not focusing on suffering.

Let's find your JOY…

> ### Find Your JOY
>
> In order to help you think of your purpose, start compiling a list of things that make you happy, that are healthy, and serve you.
>
> What has you smiling?
>
> Jot it all down.
>
> Now look at the list.
>
> What are the one or two things that you can focus on that will add more depth and meaning to your life.

Live your purpose

Yes... NOW! Life is too short not to. The next chapter will speak on action, but this section is geared on the *Why* behind things. It is about living your life on purpose; for that, you must know what your purpose is and, more importantly, *WHY* you want the things you do. There's a story of a terrible fire in an apartment complex. Fortunately, the firemen got there quickly and were able to evacuate most of the residents. A frantic mom comes running, *"Billy, Billy, where's my son?"* Her son was asleep, but woke up when he heard the screams. Billy was all by himself and didn't know what to do. He was only six years old. The fireman said to the woman, *"I'm sorry, ma'am,"* indicating he couldn't save the child. At this point, mom took a fireman's outfit and ran straight into the fire without any hesitation. She had no idea HOW she would get her son out; she just knew she had to.

The air was thick with smoke by this time, and flames had consumed the building. She screamed his name, and he answered. Thank G-

d he was still alive! She ran as fast as her legs would take her and pushed down the door almost with unbridled strength. She found him huddled down in the bathroom. She scooped him up into her coat and again ran as if her life (and her son's) depended on it (which it did). Miraculously, they made it out. The police officers and firemen were shocked to see the mother and son.

The story tells us that there is an eternal flame inside us all, our own fire that can ignite when the time arises. This fire propels us forward. The flame can become dull when we are hounded by the thoughts that we can't do something. The thoughts showed up in our childhood with such words as: *"Whaddya thinkin' boy, you're not smart enough!" "You need money for that," "Sorry, kid. You're not good enough."* We can get beat down to submission, but if we know that there is a burning desire inside all of us, it can help us get back up— like Rocky, Martin Luther King, Gandhi, and Nelson Mandela. We can prevail.

Remember, our brain is not designed to make us happy. It is designed to keep us safe. It is programmed to do the things we have always done, and it is wired to always "play it safe." Unfortunately, following the same old pattern rarely ever leads to a life of passion or fulfillment. Things can get boring really fast, and we can lose meaning as well as a sense of direction. Do you know where we can find the juice in life? It is when we step out of our comfort zone.

That is Dream BIG. When you do, rewards can manifest. All of us had dreams as children. What did you want to be when you were growing up? I know my dad told me I would be a doctor and my sister a lawyer— a Jewish parent's wish. However, when you are five, you may have other plans. I thought of myself as a baton twirler or maybe a vet. My sister wanted to own a candy store— only she liked candy so much she would probably eat all the inventory! My four-year-old niece tells me she wants to be a Doctor, a Fufu Cooker and a Rock Star as she extends her right arm and bows! I would say, *"Don't give up on your desires."*

At the same time, I would emphasize action is key. What are you doing to prepare?

My Legacy

What do you want your legacy to be?

What do you want to be remembered by?

Here is your virtual kick in the butt to make it happen and seek a coach or mentor to guide you. These next two activities are critical to making sure you're heading in the right direction by working backwards.

What did you write down? This is the time to put the top three tasks at hand. If it's one big one, break it up into edible pieces. The goal is to achieve GREATNESS and if it's too vast for your lifetime (create small successes for momentum's sake and to keep you going).

If the goal is too small (e.g., too easy to accomplish, it does not challenge you, can be done in just a few minutes), think BIGGER. Once you get close to achieving a goal, it's important to set a new one. We need to constantly grow, lest we die. If you didn't do the assignment, please do it now. If you're driving, at least do it in your head (speak aloud) or record it after you pull over. The only time we have is NOW, and when you wait (or put something off), you may never

---

My Eulogy

Imagine someone reciting your eulogy. What would they say? Who is that person? Take time now, to write this out – yes write your own eulogy. Include the things that you want people to say about your life. The type of person they knew you to be, your accomplishments, your habits and hobbies. Are you doing the things now to get you there?

---

get to it! You might have thought too small, or perhaps your goals were so big there was no point to even starting. Please make them reasonable and specific so you can accomplish them in a realistic time frame. For the next part, write your eulogy — what matters to YOU — not just what others want for you, but what you want for yourself. What will make YOU happy and bring you ultimate joy?

Don't hold back and list everything that comes to mind. It may sound morbid; it did to me when I first received this mandatory assignment at 26-years-old in medical school at the University of North Carolina, Chapel Hill (UNC). I was young, invincible, and didn't think much about death. On a side note, UNC is pretty legendary. It was the first public university in the nation established in 1789 by William Richardson Davie.

It is where Patch Adams was filmed. Besides being ranked as one of the top universities academically, it was home to the finest coaches and athletes, including Dean Smith, and basketball and soccer phenom Michael Jordan, and Mia Hamm. It's where talent meets dedication and hard work. We are all good at something and know you can manifest your greatness. Completing this powerful exercise helped me to define my ultimate goals and create a roadmap for my future. I understood these things by working backwards.

This is where the decision to open my own holistic medical practice and write a book came from. I have since repeated this activity to make sure I am staying on track.

Now it's your turn. For both **Your Legacy & Eulogy**, go wild. Jot down everything that comes to mind. Don't hold back. Go!

Remember, _inaction is a decision_. It can leave one feeling stuck, bored, angry, and frustrated. Timothy Ferris, the author of _4-Hour Work Week_, refers to the inactive people as the 'living dead'— meaning people who are merely existing and not living. They may sit on the couch and watch TV for hours, or scroll through their social media feed or play video games, or sadly work a job they hate (or where they don't feel fulfilled).

I don't know of anyone who wants to feel this way on a conscious level. Some people give up or are afraid to even try because they don't want to fail at it. I am here to tell you to **GO FOR IT**. The best way to deal with FEAR is to FACE it. It's a lot bigger in our heads. Start with an effective plan. Have patience— anything worthwhile takes time, but know you are worth it. So, what if you mess up? Take it as a part of the learning process, because that's what it is. All our great leaders have been scared and made mistakes. No one is perfect.

"It's not that they never have fear; it's that they don't let that fear STOP them!" Tanya Gold, MD

We interrupt your next regularly scheduled chapter (Habit 2) for a very important message. It's about Laughter! The easiest way I know to BE HAPPY is to LAUGH. Here are some interesting facts about this precious gift that's already inside all of us.

The Science of Laughter

"Laughter is the shortest distance between two people."

-Victor Borge

History

People have laughed since the beginning of time. It predates words and is a universal language that transcends all cultures, allowing us to connect to the human race. As John Cleese notes*: "It's impossible to maintain any kind of distance or any sense of social hierarchy when you're just howling with laughter."* Just look at someone who is genuinely giggling and notice how that makes you feel.

Laughing began way before you and I were born. It started over 10 million years ago, before humans inhabited the planet. Our ancestral primates, the apes, made guttural noises to create social bonds and connections with their troop. The behavior of laughter was initially a way to increase the chances of survival. Those who played along had improved relationships, and were better able to cope with hardship, and remain in the clan. In other words, *"hey homie, you're one of us and can stay in the cave tonight!"*

In modern times, laughter seems to do similar things. Bringing people together can combat loneliness and is often what friendships are built upon. One sparky lady told me, "I have been married to my husband for over 50 years because he still makes me laugh!"

Found worldwide, this fun practice can unite people who disagree and help them reach more amicable solutions. I wish they'd use this technique before the Middle East peace talks and presidential debates! It would have been nice to see President Trump and Hillary Clinton sharing a good ole laugh in good spirit, rather than admonishing one another during the 2016 American Presidential debates.

Many animals smile and chuckle, including apes, chimpanzees, gorillas, and orangutans. Even dogs and rats can show us their pearly whites!

Bonobos are a special species of apes that continue to laugh through adulthood (as much as they did when they were young). They have less fighting compared with other animals of their class. Imagine if humans followed suit, and adults laughed as much as they did as kids. How would the planet fare?

Interestingly, the rhythm of these sounds *"ha ha, hee hee"* echo similar languages of the past (they are short, quick, and sweet guttural noises). Just listen to a chimp being tickled[2]– the sound is contagious. Doesn't it make you want to laugh?

Religiously Speaking

Most major world religions speak of laughter. The Bible and Quran mention laughter, encouraging the adherents of the faith to smile and laugh more. For instance, Ecclesiastes 3:1-8 states: "there is a time to weep and a time to *laugh*, a time to mourn, and a time to dance." Proverbs 17:22 says: "A merry heart doeth good as medicine." Sarah's son Isaac, called Yitzchak in Hebrew, comes from the root word "Yisacheck," which means to laugh.

Yes, Sarah was laughing that, at 90 years of age, she would bear a son to Abraham, who was 99 (virile couple! I know fertility doctors would probably like to study them). Furthermore, the Quran (53:43) says, "It is He who grants laughter and tears."

You will find some representation of laughter in modern

---

[2]2017. *Chimpanzees Playing & Laughing.*
https://www.youtube.com/watch?v=ffnyOZGB-Tc

culture, as well. Footloose (an American classic, in my opinion) is an inspiring story about cheering up the spirit. The movie is set in a small town that is hit hard when the preacher's son and some of his friends drive off a bridge and are all killed. They're listening to rock and roll when this happens. Shaw, the preacher, blames this "devil's music" as the cause of this tragedy and bans all rock and roll and dancing in the town as it can *stir up evil inclinations*.

Ren, the new kid in town from Chicago, loves to dance, play loud music, and really wants to attend his prom. In a showdown with the preacher (at the town hall meeting), Ren reads directly from the Bible, Samuel 6:14-23 *14: "And David danced before the LORD with all his might,*

15 So David and all the people of Israel brought up the Ark of the LORD with shouts of joy and the blowing of rams' horns.

16 ... When she saw King David leaping and dancing before the LORD."

I won't spoil the ending (in case you haven't seen it), but Footloose is an upbeat movie that can literally make you want to get up and dance!

The Physiology of Laughter

How does it work... Chuckling causes nitric oxide to be released. This natural chemical is what opens blood vessels, increasing blood flow to our body. The effects can last for 24 hours, or until the person gets upset (which actually narrows blood vessels).

When we crack up, these major parts of our body get involved. They are the:

1. Brain

2. Face

3. Lungs

4. Heart

5. Diaphragm (dome-shaped muscle in between the lungs and intestines)

6. Abdomen

7. Larynx (voice box)

8. Mouth

So what triggers laughter? There is a whole science behind laughing— how it starts and how it affects the human body.

Let's go through the explanations one by one.

Triggers of Laughter

Your brain perceives stimuli, or sensation, from the environment. It can be anything that you find unexpected, absurd, or funny or in a social context. For me, it was watching my stepmom try on her first pair of skis. She couldn't stand up, and as my sister and I tried to help her, all of us fell down. My dad lost it, watching us. All of us did (and that made it even harder to get up).

My husband, Drew, had a similar experience when he attempted to ski a double black diamond after a long hiatus (what he was thinking, I have no idea). Hitting the same patch of ice twice (yes, he did it again), he howled with laughter as he rolled backward down the mountain as people cheered him on from the chairlifts. He and his friends now have renamed "Regulator Johnson" (this steep ski slope at Snowbird in Salt Lake City), the *"Drew Slide."* Interestingly, falling (without getting hurt) is a common reason for folks to laugh.

Why laugh? According to psychiatrist William Fry from Stanford University, it helps us cope with hardship, a sort of 'natural painkiller,' and those witnessing a fall may feel better about their own predicament. Just watch Wipeout. Hilarious. Sometimes, participants are dressed in giant rubber suits appearing as Willy Wonka's Oompa Loompas, trying to complete a goofy slippery obstacle course as fast as they can. Because of the nature of their silly protective suits, they don't just fall, they bounce.

Surprisingly, researcher Robert Provine, who is a professor of psychology and neuroscience, found that most laughter does not follow a joke. It is very much governed by the social context.

Provine observed thousands of cases where cackling often followed random speech— even a sentence as mundane as *"Hey Johnny, whad'ya doin' here?"* made folks erupt into laughter.

In his studies, groups laughed 30 times more often compared to those who were alone. The interactions lasted longer and occurred more often with good friends than with strangers.

Gelotology

Gelotology is the field that studies laughter. It is a combination of the Greek word 'gelos' meaning laughter, and 'logy' meaning 'study of,' (maybe that makes me a gelotologist). There have been several studies done on the science of laughter. The scientist Peter Derks used an EEG (electroencephalograph scan that measures the brain's electrical activity) to show that when a person laughs, the frontal lobe of their brain gets stimulated (meaning that it lights up), as do many other areas such as the motor cortex, occipital lobe (responsible for visual processing), amygdala and hippocampus (responsible for emotions) and hypothalamus (responsible for loud, uncontrollable laughter. Do you know anyone like that?).

In the situation with my stepmom, our brain went to work once it sensed the fiasco on the ski slope, and laughter erupted. Others sensed it too, and a crowd formed joining in on the merriment. This shows how contagious giggling can be!

Once the brain decides to laugh, it signals a prolonged exhalation (recruiting the diaphragm, abdominal muscles, larynx, and facial muscles including the zygomatic major muscle which is responsible for raising the top lip into your stunning smile). That creates a welcoming sound that invites others to join in. Amazingly, all of this happens in a matter of seconds.

In a nutshell:

- The brain perceives *something* that triggers laughter (or we can trigger it consciously, the premise of laughter yoga.)

- Multiple areas in the brain light up

- This elicits a strong exhale (making a guttural noise through our voice box) better known as the proverbial giggle

- The whole body can be involved as the cascade of hormones gets released, and our muscles can relax (any pain can be reduced) for up to an hour or more depending on how long we laugh.

The whole body can be involved in amusement. We can perceive laughter from our various senses— we see it, feel it (as when we are tickled), smell it (as when someone burps or farts which cracks people up. I know it's disgusting, but it happens, just part of being human. (My three-year-old niece says she burped her tushy!) So, the brain perceives a trigger to cackle using one or the other sense. The left side of your brain perceives stimuli (which can be something funny or a social connection). If it is a joke, you may see the irony in it. The right side of the brain processes it as funny (or not). Then the signals go to the amygdala for the right emotional response (which includes feeling pleasure).

As for the body, laughter causes a deep exhalation coming from the throat. Mirth can spread like a virus among friends. When you laugh, others laugh too! By roaring with glee, you give them permission to do the same. Guffawing helps rid your body of stale air, bringing in fresh oxygen. It engages multiple muscles in your face to contract and relax, beginning in the first 10 seconds, including the zygomatic arch, which causes the upper lip to rise -the universal sign of endearment. ♥ Hearty, genuine laughter stimulates the eyes to cringe and may produce tears of joy. This can also

---

Look Younger!

Take a selfie before and after 15 minutes of laughter.

True beauty appears when we laugh & smile.

---

increase blood flow to the face giving it a natural glow! Authentic laughter can erupt spontaneously (or intentionally). Either way, it feels glorious when it comes from the belly and heart. The full benefits can last an hour or more if it is conducted for at least 15 minutes.[3]

Many parts of the brain get stimulated:

- Prefrontal cortex

- Accumbens

- Motor cortex

- Amygdala

Laughing for Benefit

Are there medical benefits to laughing? The simple answer is yes! For those suffering from anxiety, depression, or anger, learning to laugh can seem foreign. The nice part is that laughter is innate. We don't really need to *learn* anything, but just remember and give ourselves permission to move forward in the act. Playfulness helps. Laughter yoga is an exercise program that cultivates joy. It teaches

---

[3]Khamsi, Roxanne. 2005. "Laughter Boosts Blood-Vessel Health." *Nature* news050307-4. doi: 10.1038/news050307-4.

participants how to play again. They may start with clapping their hands and collectively say, "Very good. Very good. Yeah!" The delight becomes contagious, and even those who cannot see or hear can join in on the fun. It does not need to be taught.

Research confirms a multitude of benefits from laughing.

1. Lowers stress by reducing cortisol
2. Improves blood pressure and blood sugar
3. Strengthens our core

Laughter is one of the best ab workouts ever, AND it's FUN! One German study showed it worked deeper abdominal muscles, more so than crunches.[4] Doing this for at least 15 minutes a day can increase the blood flow to the brain and have a sustained effect on our body.

Heart disease is the leading cause of death worldwide. Research shows people who suffer from heart disease are 40% less likely to be *light-hearted*![5] According to Dr. Miller, *"The recommendation for a healthy heart may one day be —*

---

[4] JMot Behav. 2014;46(1):33-7.doi10.1080/00222895.2013.844091. Epub 2013 Nov 18.
[5] "Humor Helps Your Heart? How?" Retrieved from https://www.heart.org/HEARTORG/Conditions/More/MyHeartandStrokeNews/Humor-helps-your-heart-How_UCM_447039_Article.jsp

exercise, eat right and laugh a few times a day.[6]

There is growing evidence that laughter boosts the immune system— increasing natural killer cells.[7] It can even help cancer patients feel better and start cracking jokes— "No need for a haircut or shampoo."

One study by cardiologist Michael Miller, at the University of Maryland Medical center, showed those who watched the comedy show "Saturday Night Live" for 15 minutes opened their blood vessels by 22% (increasing blood flow.) Consequently, those who watched the serious film "Saving Private Ryan" narrowed their blood vessels by 35%, reducing flow. [8]

There was another study demonstrating the relationship between laughing and memory. Older adults who cackled scored higher on their memory tests.[9] This applied to other

---

[6] "BBC News | HEALTH | Laughter 'Protects the Heart.'" Retrieved from (http://news.bbc.co.uk/2/hi/health/1024713.stm).

[7] Bennett, Mary Payne, and Cecile Lengacher. 2009. "Humor and Laughter May Influence Health IV. Humor and Immune Function." *Evidence-Based Complementary and Alternative Medicine : ECAM* 6(2):159–64. doi: 10.1093/ecam/nem149

[8] Miller, Michael, and William F. Fry. 2009. "The Effect of Mirthful Laughter on the Human Cardiovascular System." *Medical Hypotheses* 73(5):636–39. doi: 10.1016/j.mehy.2009.02.044.

[9] Bains, Gurinder Singh, Lee S. Berk, Noha Daher, Everett Lohman, Ernie Schwab, Jerrold Petrofsky, and Pooja Deshpande. 2014. "The Effect of Humor on Short-Term Memory in Older Adults: A New Component for Whole-Person

age groups too. Students in a stats class who received humor during their lessons outperformed the non-humor group on the final exam by 10%.[10] Try this out before a big exam or presentation– or you can even take it a step further and use it while preparing for these endeavors (or to help put you in the mood.) As for mood disorders, symptoms of anxiety, and depression, for example, can wane with a regular dose of laughter.[11] [12] This makes sense as our brain is hardwired to respond positively to mirth. This activity can complement traditional medical treatments, including antidepressants, which some studies have raised questions over their effectiveness and whether they are even better than placebo.[13] I am not pointing this out to have patients necessarily stop their medications cold turkey but consider

---

Wellness." *Advances in Mind-Body Medicine* 28(2):16–24.https://www.ncbi.nlm.nih.gov/pubmed/24682001

[10] "Humor, Laughter, Learning, and Health! A Brief Review | Advances in Physiology Education." Retrieved from https://www.physiology.org/doi/full/10.1152/advan.00030.2017

[11] "Stress Relief from Laughter? It's No Joke - Mayo Clinic." Retrieved from (https://www.mayoclinic.org/healthy-lifestyle/stress-management/in-depth/stress-relief/art-20044456

[12] "Mayo Mindfulness: Laughter for Stress Relief Is No Joke." *Https://Newsnetwork.Mayoclinic.Org/*. Retrieved from https://newsnetwork.mayoclinic.org/discussion/mayo-mindfulness-stress-relief-with-laughter-is-no-joke/.

[13] Newman, Tim 2019. "Do Antidepressants Work Better than Placebo?" Retrieved from (https://www.medicalnewstoday.com/articles/325767).

complementing their treatments if what they're doing is not working, or they want to see if it can work even better. In addition, some patients suffer from intolerable side effects from these medications, so it's nice to have options. Have you ever met a person taking antidepressants for a while who was still depressed? Francis was a patient of mine who *tried it all* (years of various antidepressants, mood stabilizers, anxiety meds, and even ECT (shock therapy) and was unresponsive to it all. Find out what happened to her with some cheering up during our visit. You'll meet her later under the last habit on Health (YES, I want you to read the entire book!).

Laughter with few side effects is affordable and can be added to almost any medical regiment. According to Wayne Dyer, *"It is impossible to laugh and be upset at the same time."*

Don't Be Fooled

There is a condition known as 'smiling depression' where people may smile and laugh on the *outside* but feel physically distraught on the inside. If they seem upset (even if they're cackling), keep probing and let them know you're there for them and care. You may suggest professional help. The laughing and smiling we describe here is cultivating self-love. It's coming from the inside and is heartfelt and genuine. We don't want you to just 'fake it until you make it.' We want you to *feel it to believe it!*

What Laughter Does

"Anything you dread, try laughing instead."

-Dr. Tanya Gold

Giggling not only increases the blood flow and reduces cortisol levels, but it also acts as our body's natural opiate, relieving tension, and decreasing pain through a giant surge of endorphins. This fun behavior allows one to be more resistant to stress and disease. Studies show those who laugh regularly show improved quality of life.

Think about it, if you are laughing so hard your eyes tear up, and your belly hurts (in a good way), how likely is it for you to focus on your worries? ☺ The tears of laughter are different than the tears of sorrow. Allen Klein, the author of *"Learning to Laugh, when you Feel like Crying: Embracing Life After Loss,"* reveals, *"Laughter helps us transcend our suffering; crying does not."*

Tears of sadness turn us inward; we cry and feel sorry for ourselves. Laughter, on the other hand, focuses us outward. Laughter expands our vision and gives us a new way of seeing our situation. *"The laughing person,"* notes author Helmuth Plessner, *"is open to the world."*

The crying person, on the other hand, only sees his world and his suffering. Perhaps this is why one Yiddish proverb notes that "laughter can be heard farther than weeping." Who would you rather spend time with, someone who brings you down, or one who uplifts you?

How to Prevail

Think of something challenging in your life. Imagine your hand as the challenge and put it in front of your face. Now, cover your eyes with this hand as you focus on this difficult time. Take a deep breath in and smile (do it three times). Slowly move your hand away from your eyes and look around. Now, visualize yourself overcoming this challenge. This metaphor is what laughter does. It can offer you a *new* perspective, making lemonade out of lemons. When my key got stuck in my office door, and I was running late, I began to laugh and snort. Instead of continuing to pull (and possibly break the key and make myself even later), I immediately called the super, who got some WD-40.

By laughing, my state was relaxed. Instead of focusing on the problem (and getting riled up), I focused on the solution and felt calmer. Chuckling made it easier to ask myself, "How can I overcome?" The creative solution popped up instantly.

Laugh for No Reason

Because if we *wait* to laugh until something is funny, we may never get to it. To achieve the most benefit laugh for at least 15 minutes.

It may seem weird to laugh for no reason, but newsflash: we ALL have done it! Babies begin smiling at six weeks, and then begin laughing from the age of 3 to 4 months, way before their verbal skills develop. So, in essence, when we were still "goo goo ga ga-ing" in the crib, we were cracking ourselves up, even though we didn't get the joke!

How did we get so darn serious as adults? Is our culture responsible for this? As infants, we were funny, even to ourselves. What do adults typically do when they see a baby gurgling and cooing? Sure, they may smile and mimic them. In Qatar (near Saudi Arabia), I saw a man dressed in a long white robe (thawb) with a black rope and scarf around his head (keffiyeh). While his daughter was running around, he put on her tiny pink sunglasses. When she caught sight of him, she ran up to him, smiled, and they both giggled.

As we mature, we may get the notion we *must* be serious and *have a reason* to crack up. This may start in school or at a religious service where people are taught to be quiet, sit still, and cackling may be frowned upon during a lesson or sermon.

We may have been told "be serious," "act your age" (what's that?), "get to work," "wipe that grin off your face boy," "this is no time for foolishness," "that's enough fun for one day" (who says) and "buck up soldier." How often are we encouraged to "BE silly," "have *MORE* fun" and "Keep laughing?"

Painful Procedures

Have you thought of what role laughter can play during painful procedures? One pediatric oncology nurse told me her 6-year-old patient asked if he could laugh while his blood was being drawn. Unlike the other patients, who kicked and screamed, Brian said he barely felt anything. It is not a placebo effect. When you laugh, endorphins, including natural pain killers, get released. This makes painful procedures, including natural childbirth, more bearable.

Can you enjoy childbirth?

One of my colleague's wives practiced *hypnobirthing.* It means reframing the birth into a positive experience. Contractions are called surges, and you are taught to breathe deeply, like Lamaze. After delivery, this colleague's wife began chuckling. Puzzled, the doctor asked, *"Why are you laughing?"* She said, *"I am laughing because you said this wouldn't work!"*

On YouTube, there is a video of a woman who is cracking up during her entire delivery. What if pregnant women were taught to **expect a positive experience**, and laughter played a pivotal role during labor? I know it may sound ludicrous now, but so did launching a rocket into space, or soaring high in the sky. Now many people fly to Europe without giving it a second thought. Just think of how an airplane weighing several tons can lift off and fly thousands of feet above the ground still amazes me! It teaches us that almost anything is possible. If cackling comes with little side effects and great rewards, why not try it? What do you have to lose? It does get easier with practice. As a woman, I know I would rather laugh while giving birth than scream and cry.

Empowered Meaning

I am operating under the assumption that you *WANT* to feel better. I have never met a patient (or anyone) who wanted to feel lousy! So, how about developing an empowered meaning for *anything* that happens to you and doing whatever it takes to get better in a healthy way. Laughter is the road map. It can teach you *HOW* to lighten the discouragement, anger, or agony by offering a new perspective.

Giggling can help us break FREE and *ask* the right questions. How can I grow? What can I learn? How can I celebrate this person's life (in the case of someone dying or completing their life)? How can I be a better human being (dad, mom, husband, wife, teenager)? Laughter can lead the way– which will not only make you feel better but others as well. It can energize you and teach you how to keep going, no matter what. The key to any good plan is Action (which brings us to the next habit)!

We now return to our regularly scheduled Chapters. Hope you enjoyed one of my favorite topics! ♥

Habit #2— Act Getting Started

"Well begun is half done."

-Aristotle

Think of when you first learned to walk. I know it was a long time ago and you may have no recollection of it. Even so, think of a baby wobbling and plopping down, only to get back up and try it again, and again, and then again, until one day, they start walking— all on their own and without falling. Woohoo! That was you once. You didn't give up. It is safe to say that not giving up is the reason why most people walk in this world. You don't even have to think about it now (just like you don't have to think much if you have been driving a car for a while). Sure, there will be tough times, but you can still do it.

It takes the same attitude to be happy. Listen, you picked this book up for a reason. Maybe you know me, or perhaps you want your life to be different and happier with more joy, meaning, and purpose in it. Whatever the reason, everything starts with YOU! You need to decide to "bring it."

Laughter is the simplest way I know to get you there. I'm not trying to make light of your situation. There is pain and suffering in the world and laughter can help. I can't say I understand what you're personally going through. All I can do is speak from my perspective and share stories of those rising up from the most dire of circumstances. Looking at these incredible people with their amazing stories, I believe we can all transcend the bad situations of our lives and become pros at laughing (or at least much better)!

Now, you may say, "Dr. Gold, I don't have much to laugh at." I hear you. Let's think of it this way. If you think of ALL the good things that have happened to you, how does that make you feel? It's all about perspective. A 99-year-old powerlifter who I work out with tells me often, "It's a good day! Why? Because I woke up on the right side of the green."

If you ever wake up on the *wrong* side of the bed, go back to bed, and wake up on the right side. Either way, remember you woke up!

We must appreciate all the gifts we _**do**_ have: we are breathing, our heart is beating, we can see, walk, smell, hear, taste, and YES because WE are here. If things are not working out, we can use them as learning opportunities for growth. This book is NOT about denying your emotions, but figuring out beneficial ways for you to be happy. You have every right to feel the way you do. You are just choosing to feel good anyway. You are deciding to lighten up rather than feel weighed down. Anger and stress can tighten the body while joy relaxes it. That's what I do in traffic. Instead of getting huffy, I start rockin' it out with upbeat music and ask myself, "How do I want to feel?"

Timeout

Do you get mad? All of us have. It's part of being human. Anger usually stems from feeling hurt, which comes from a feeling of loss. In relationships, you may feel that the other person is not valuing you or meeting your needs. When you get mad, you waste precious energy on someone else. In other words, you give them power over you. You let them push your buttons and control your state. Instead, you can take charge of your emotions and decide how you want to feel. It gets easier with practice. You don't need to wait for the situation to escalate or even occur. *You can STOP it!*

The S.TO.P. Method

1.Smile and take 3 deep breaths

2.Take control & empower yourself (make your best superhero pose)

3.Out loud state with conviction: "I GOT this!

I am in charge of my emotions, I CAN Overcome!"

4.Pause: You may even call a "time out"— and let off some steam with a punching bag, pillow, walk or run. Sometimes a good roar, laugh or cold shower can help. I also like fun music.

5.Yes, timeout until you feel relaxed. It's ok to admit "I'm upset, give me a minute." A lot better than saying or doing something you'll regret.

6.Daily meditative practices i.e. tai chi and yoga strengthen your resolve to a calmer state, and you can learn to "STOP it" through practice.

*As a physician, I remind my patients they are NOT alone, they are loved, and recommend they seek professional help as they need it.

When you earnestly say with an empowering movement, "I am in control of my feelings, I am in charge, and I get to decide how I want to feel," it's amazing how your brain goes "okay." Understand no one can control your thoughts except YOU! Remember, your mind (especially your subconscious mind) doesn't know right from wrong. It only knows what you tell it. On a side note, that's how violence can continue. The perpetrator may feel that what they are doing is righteous, even if it hurts innocent lives. That's how genocide continues, and it will continue until we understand this.

You CAN think for yourself. I always wondered what would have happened if more people stood up to Hitler and said, "No, we will NOT do this. This is wrong." I know this may sound farfetched, especially for those people who find themselves in the throes of war, but some brave souls did this in their own way. They are the heroes, some of who are mentioned in an inspiring book titled *"Those Who Save Us"* by Jenna Blum.

The Nazis not only killed many Jews but also those that were different, including but not limited to same-sex couples and those with disabilities. It's interesting in a tiny country of Denmark, almost all the Jews lived. They were able to escape to Sweden with the assistance of the Danish resistance movement and the help of many of its civilians, a brave act for which they were rewarded.

As you manage your state better, you can propel yourself forward faster in accomplishing your goals (less likely to get sidetracked) and remain focused. If someone upsets you, you won't let that key you off and fixate on that for the rest of your day or week (letting everyone know what happened and "can you believe that guy?") <u>Prolonged stays in emotions that DON'T serve you, tax the body and drain your energy.</u> FREE YOURSELF! You DO have a choice! Don't let these unserving emotions hold you back. **Do you want to be right or happy?**

To the Finish Line

How I finally got this book done was simple: I decided to write it and took massive action. I had been telling people for years I would write a book. I even got a book title in my head, but then I changed it. Nothing happened for a long time because I procrastinated. I had no formal action plan. I would just sit and write when I felt like it.

Well, life doesn't work that way. You don't always feel like going to school or work, or tending to the kids, but you do it because it needs to get done. The same goes for your dreams. Sometimes they're the last thing we get to (or we don't), and we wonder why we feel miserable or unfulfilled. Once I simplified the process and hired a coach to keep me accountable for my action plan and help me stay focused, my dreams started coming true. How many people leave this world with a great idea or a great book or song, still inside them? I suspect a lot. I've met many folks who've told me a brilliant idea, and years later, when I ask them about it, I find nothing has been done, or they may have long forgotten about it. Why?

They may have been afraid or felt unworthy or not felt they had the means. That was me at first; I wasn't confident enough to believe I could write well or feel anyone would read this book. But I overcame with a change in mindset. Through the L.A.U.G.H. method that I am teaching you in this book, I learned I could accomplish anything I set my mind to, including writing a valuable self-help book. What motivates me is realizing how many more people I can impact versus sharing this knowledge 'one patient at a time.'

What separates someone from being successful or not is taking reasonable action. Everything you do is not going to work out, but you can adjust and tweak it along the way. **GO FOR IT!** Honestly, I've never met anyone who regretted a sincere call to action. Either way, they've learned or grown, and that can be you. When you don't act, you deprive not only yourself, but others of your brilliance. The world will never benefit from your vision, or you may get disillusioned or jaded if you feel someone "has stolen your idea" because they acted quicker. That's ok. Do it anyway. There are tons of duplicates. Just think of Lyft and Uber. You can always expand upon your talent or make it better or guess what— there will just be one more brand of shoes!

Action is key

When I hear people complain, I ask them, "What are YOU DOING about it?" If it's something at the YMCA where I teach yoga, I ask them if they have a solution and have they spoken to a manager, or if it's related to politics, the same thing, what's your suggestion and who have you contacted? As Joseph McClendon III puts it, "talk is cheap." He is the no-nonsense author of "Putting a S.T.O.P. to It."

His book and CDs provide valuable advice on how to make your life work. He should know as he was once homeless and now is a successful businessman. Don't be selfish, share your ideas, act upon them so that others may benefit, and you as well (because it can become your legacy!)

I'm no different from you. You have a gift— a flame, a passion inside of you. You have a purpose.

Are you living it?

If not, you must start taking action. You won't regret it. As my dad said, *"You don't want to be at the end of your life, wondering 'what if?'."*

Legendary peak performance coach Tony Robbins inspires millions to "live with passion." He speaks about the 6 Human Needs: The need for

1. Certainty (to know that you're safe or secure financially)
2. Uncertainty or variety (no need for Taco Tuesdays, may mix it up a bit)
3. Significance (to know you matter and are important)
4. Love/connection (people care about you)
5. Growth (continuing to learn)

6. Contribution (giving back)

What are your top two needs? When at least two of your most important needs are being met (at a high level), you can have a satisfying life. When you have all six performing well, it can be extraordinary. Tony also mentions why many people don't have their dream life. It can be their limiting beliefs, "their story" or self-talk in their heads for why it isn't so. All of us have predominant questions we tend to ask ourselves. And as you can imagine, if you ask yourself over and over, "why am I such a screw-up," it's not hard to see why you might be. What if you asked, "how can I make my life work, how can I make this an amazing day, how can I overcome, or what can I learn from this?" Your brain looks for answers to the questions you give it.

So, if you ask, "why can't I ever make enough money" or "I can never afford that," you likely never will because your brain is focusing on the problem rather than a solution. The great part is you can simply change your question to "how can I make MORE money?" (yes, change your self-talk) and with practice quell these unserving thoughts in your head and then take proper action, of course. Is your self-talk limiting or expanding? If you're heading in the right direction, you know you are on the right track. Tony asks people to never say 'I should do this' or 'I should do that' (i.e., "I should eat better, and exercise more, or I should lose weight"). Don't *should* all over yourself! Wavering is not going to get you anywhere. Just Do it!

Instead state boldly, "I **WILL** eat better, lose weight and exercise," and commit with a trainer or coach. It's rare to have everything be perfect. Do you know when the time to **ACT** is? Correct **NOW**! That's all the time you got.

* On a side note: If you read some negative press about the people I speak about in this book, no one is perfect. I'm not condoning inappropriate behavior, but I don't want to discount all the great things they have done either: helping people live better lives, become better parents, and providing food for the hungry.

I used to lie to myself and say that I'll do it later. Procrastination feeds on itself, and it's easy to get caught up, becoming more complacent and comfortable. It's like having a nice cozy couch. How likely are you to get up once you're relaxed, watching some TV, and enjoying a nice beverage and snack? But you need to get up and get to work or get to play, or don't sit down until the work gets done. Do what it takes to achieve your desired goals.

Also, don't worry about what it's going to look like to other people or what they will say about it. Again, that's their problem, not yours. ***Your job is to get your dreams done and enjoy the process.***

What if you feel you can't afford your dreams?

Money problems can be the source of much angst. Why not instead focus on abundance and attracting wealth? Let go of telling yourself you don't have "enough money." If you keep telling yourself this, will you? This "money poor attitude," I am speaking about comes from my own personal experience, when my husband and I almost went bankrupt. Once we changed our psychology to a growth mindset, the money began to flow in, as did our happiness. We fought less and were less stressed about how we were going to pay the bills and whether we would lose our home.

Lacking money is a problem, but not the solution. You feel what you focus on. What if you focused on what you want? If you want more money, how can you begin attaining it? With the internet, there are many ways to earn money. If you have a worthy cause and a plan, make it known, so you can attract investors. I have many friends using "GOFUNDME" including my sister who used it to obtain a scooter. One of my friends financed her trip to Israel with a raffle for "the ultimate car wash" at her synagogue. She only had to clean one car. There are many agencies out there to help, or you can save up. That's what I did for my business. I never took out any loans.

Once a project is done, think about how your life will change and how you will feel once you have finally acted, and how confident you will become. You then have the story of how you got it done, rather than harboring any regrets over why you didn't.

There is usually someone who has accomplished what you are attempting to do. Model their success.

My Hero

My dad is a man of action and not many words. His business advice to me, "make money." He immigrated to this country from the West Indies at the age of 16. He stuttered, which is why I think he didn't speak much, but he got help. His mentor believed in him and instilled not only better pronunciation, but confidence in his ability to make things happen. My father lived the American dream acquiring monetary wealth and, fortunately, happiness through his easy-going attitude and loving family. I believe in YOU. You CAN make things happen. Even if we haven't met (and if we haven't, I hope we do someday), know there is a reason you picked up this book. You may be looking to take your life to the next level— help more people— and do more good in this world. Whatever the case, your potential is infinite… never give up and do what you can to live your life with passion.

Getting back to my dad, he worked hard. Coming to this country with barely any money, he filled his pockets with dreams. He put himself through school while working full time as a security guard at Chase Manhattan Bank in New York City. He went to night school at NYU and earned his degree in accounting. *"Pops, when did you sleep?"* *"In the bathroom, until they found me."*

He opened TRIN Brokerage (Taxes, Real-estate, & INsurance) in the early 70s, and only recently sold it. Knowing not to put all his eggs in one basket, he acquired several properties and began to race horses (after he got paid with them from a client). Not afraid of hard work (and used to it from his earlier days), he could easily spend 14 hours at the office, even longer during tax season, where he sometimes stayed over.

Like the millionaire next door, he saved and saved. He drove the same sky-blue Volvo, which became my car until it died, and we didn't take our first holiday until I was 10. Gradually, he built up his empire.

Working so hard and not eating well or exercising began to take a toll on my dad's health, including a huge bulge in his midline.

After my father's blood pressure skyrocketed, in his early 40's, his doctor asked him, "do you want to see your daughters grow up?" Thankfully, my dad took this seriously and began running. My sister Marissa and I jumped at the opportunity to join him on the track, because we barely saw him except in the mornings (when he made us breakfast).

Our first race

Van Cortlandt Park in the Bronx on a beautiful fall day was our first cross-country race, a 5K family run (3.1 miles). Adrenaline pumping through me, I went out pretty quickly but felt good. Halfway in, I reached an incline. It seemed to never end. I found out later it was called Cemetery Hill (appropriately named as I thought I might die trying to reach the top). My legs felt like lead all of a sudden, and I began panting, having trouble catching my breath. Marathoners call it "hitting the wall." My brain just told me, "to give up; it's too hard." It didn't help that I looked up, and my 10-year-old mind saw this monstrous mountain. I began to feel tears well up. By this time, my pace slowed down to a crawl, and I began looking back. I finally saw my dad. *"Great, he'll walk with me,"* I thought. Crying by the time he caught up with me, I blubbered out, *"Dad, I can't do this. I'm so tired."* *"So, stop,"* he responded simply.

I smiled and did what he said. I thought he would join me, but he continued on. When he was a few yards ahead of me, he turned around and smirked. *"Oh, no way! I can't let my dad beat me!"* I forgot all about the pain and started running again with all my might.

Grit

This is a good time to check-in. How do you deal with challenges? Do you tend to give up easily or dig deep or do something in between? There's an insightful book on this subject called "Grit," by Angela Duckworth. Grit is your ability to stay the course even if it's hard, "not give up" and persevere for your passions for years, recognizing **failure is not a permanent condition** (and you can continue until you succeed). "Start Up Nation" by Dan Senor is another great book on this topic. It speaks about how the Israeli companies flourished even after the stock market crash in 2008.

Often the ones who struggle the most, but persevere, grow the most. The ones who seem to have it easy, especially early on, may be more hard pressed later. For example, my brother is brilliant and was reading encyclopedias when he was a toddler. However, now as an adult, he's become a late bloomer when it comes to leaving the nest for good and working on his own. He's spoken of a passion, but I have yet to see any commitment towards it on his part.

Carol Dweck, professor of psychology at Stanford University, speaks about the "growth mindset" and how you can build grit. All of us have the ability to be tough (to be strong and powerful and believe in ourselves). We just need to practice it. It's like in the movie "Police Academy," where squeaky soft-spoken Hooks (the sweet black woman) belts out, "don't move dirtbag," by the end of her police training.

All of us have this powerful voice inside ourselves, that can be accessed through our passions. Within us all, we have the ability to *decide* to be happy, and all of us deserve that.

When humans feel good, they tend to smile and laugh. By the same token, how often one smiles and laughs can determine how good they feel. Just think of anything that has you burst out laughing, how does that make you feel? F*ckin awesome, I know. Fortunately, you can choose how much happiness or joy you have in your life. Laughter can be the bridge.

*Please excuse the profanity. It's not to be vulgar. But when people curse, it can hit visceral parts of us. Awesome is a nice word, but when you add the profanity f*ckin, it adds new meaning. I don't curse all the time, but words matter, and if it can help put a smile on your face or help you feel MORE and better understand what I am trying to say, it's worth it.

Powerful words (and adding variety to your life) can jolt your nervous system and wake you up from the ho-hum days, which can lead to boredom. Why not add more healthy excitement? It doesn't have to cost much. It can be as simple as having a family picnic in your living room, jumping up and down screaming with glee, rocking it out to your favorite song, or having a pillow fight, tickle fight or water fight, or just being playful, i.e., dance-off. Whatever it is — choose to have fun!! No matter what age you are, your life can be an adventure!!

Happiness vs. Joy

In this book, I am using happiness and joy interchangeably but there are important distinctions.

As I alluded to before, happiness is fleeting. It's conditional— based on getting that prestigious job or position or getting that expensive car or home you've always dreamed of. It can seem it's never quite enough. Joy is long-lasting. It comes from within and is unconditional (not based on anything except a choice to feel better because YOU are here, and you are amazing)! That's what I want you to feel.

Joy can also come from the love you get from raising children (yes, I am talking about the sweet parts, not when they go "boy or girl crazy" and then drive you crazy or throw a tantrum, although now you can throw one too (check out YouTube 'drgoldfunyoga'— Tantrum Yoga (No, NOT Tantra Yoga, although that would be nice too!).

Joy can come from many things, and I find it often when I volunteer. Helping someone in dire need makes me feel wonderful. I sometimes feel I am getting more out of it than they are. For example, my little sister Minnie from Big Brothers Big Sisters (a mentoring program) has continued to ask me when my book is coming out! I finally wrote the darn thing, so she'd stop bugging me! ☺

Joy can also come from spending time with your loved ones. One hospice nurse told me about how many of her patients wished they spent more time with their families, instead of at the office. Life is short. LIVE IT!!

How Happy Are You?

Take this questionnaire to find out.

Please answer honestly (circle your responses)

		Almost never	Seldom	Some-times	Often	Always
1	I'm living my purpose	1	2	3	4	5
2	I smile often	1	2	3	4	5
3	I laugh a lot	1	2	3	4	5
4	I am playful	1	2	3	4	5
5	I'm not afraid to poke fun at myself (in a healthy manner)	1	2	3	4	5
6	I have close connections with others	1	2	3	4	5
7	I love myself	1	2	3	4	5
8	I take care of my health	1	2	3	4	5

		Almost Never	Seldom	Some-times	Often	Always
9	I handle adversity with ease	1	2	3	4	5
10	My stress levels are manageable	1	2	3	4	5
11	I am full of energy and life	1	2	3	4	5
12	I often perform random acts of kindness	1	2	3	4	5
13	I live with passion and enthusiasm	1	2	3	4	5
14	I can laugh at my mistakes	1	2	3	4	5
15	I do not laugh at other people's expense (engage in cruel jokes that hurt others)	1	2	3	4	5

		Almost Never	Seldom	Some-times	Often	Always
16	I can see something positive in most things that happen	1	2	3	4	5
17	I take "ME" time	1	2	3	4	5
18	I have a great sense of humor	1	2	3	4	5
19	I make time for hobbies	1	2	3	4	5
20	I am living without regrets	1	2	3	4	5

Your Laughter Quotient Score

76-100 Great. Continue to soar and share your cheer with others. Know there's no endpoint to your joy.

50-75 You're getting there. Keep making progress by practicing the exercises and check out the educational modules (see end of book). Commit to laughing regularly with a mentor or with a laughter group. Seek help as you need it.

0-49 An opportunity for growth. Focus on what tickles your funny bone and commit to laughing regularly because it helps change perspective and puts a bounce in your stride. Find an accountability partner, mentor, or join the laughter hotline or Skype group. Joining regular laughers makes it easier for you to stay on track, just like having a coach or teammate. I also created education modules to help you in this area (see the end of the book). Please seek professional help as you need it.

There is always hope and know that you CAN improve! As you play the games and apply the principles, take this questionnaire again and re-evaluate your scores. I bet they improve.

Start

Beginning anything new can be tough, especially if you are going through a rough time and have a lot on your plate. Those who have trained for a marathon — especially when they weren't in shape — know it begins with the first step, which is often the hardest.

Remember, laughter is NOT a spectator sport. You need to participate to get the full benefits! This book is not for the faint of heart. It's meant to be applied. Like operating a car, you can't merely learn from a simulation — as Sheldon Cooper from the 'Big Bang' tried to do — you need to actually get in and drive. Sheldon, a brilliant scientist, could figure out almost any complex physics equation, but not the wheel. Become the driver of your own life, and learn how to master your thoughts, so they serve you. Otherwise, you become their servant.

It's a choice. Through the key formula that I will describe here, you can succeed. I am using the acronym, DBAC, to help you remember it. It stands for Decide, Believe, Act, and Commit.

YOU CAN do this. You have come this far in the book. What some surveys show is that many people don't read past the first chapter and here you are in the second chapter– which, in my opinion, is one of the most important, because this is really where we get to experience the benefits, especially with long-term practice.

Success Formula— D.B.A.C.

D.B.A.C— Decide, Believe, Act, and Commit.

To **decide** means to cut off other possibilities, like when you choose vanilla ice cream over chocolate!

You need to **believe** you can do this, because if you do not, how likely are you to succeed? Olympic gold medalists often visualize themselves winning gold way before they actually do.

You can also have the desire and belief, but if you don't **Act,** nothing will change. There are many great inventions and books (that we will never get to see or read about) because they died with the person. They thought about it, but never *did* anything about it!

Commitment is having the patience and diligence to stick with it no matter what. It will get challenging, but others have done it, and so can you. It takes the attitude of "never giving up." All of us have this inside of us; it just needs to be cultivated. Think of the things that you followed through on in your life already. It may be raising your kids. (You didn't get rid of them, although you may have thought about it, especially when they became *sassy* teenagers!)

Now going back to one of your first assignments, what did you write for your eulogy? What do you want to be remembered by? What do you want your legacy to be? If you didn't DO the assignment (you are in the right place), please do it NOW. YES NOW! If you did, good job! Please look at what you wrote. What is the **ONE** thing you want to accomplish? Focus. Visualize yourself going after that goal and completing it. Now, what do you need to begin or, if you are in the midst of doing it, what do you need to continue? If you got stuck, what help can you get to accomplish this task? Remember, it's NOT TOO LATE (unless you continue to wait and let it be). Do it NOW! You will feel so much better! Once you tackle that, go to the next thing on your list. If you complete all these goals one by one, you may start over with writing your new legacy.

It is amazing how we can evolve. Once you accomplish something, your brain says, "Now, what else can I do?" There is no endpoint. What you can conceive, you can achieve! Your accomplishments are limitless. *You are incredible and have infinite capabilities*! Your brain can memorize and learn far more than what researchers thought was possible, with just some key strategies.

We are all in different places, and we will begin from wherever you are at, so no need to fret. It is sometimes those that come from the greatest heartache who can find the sweetest joy. Why? Because they need it the most and are ready to start on their new path.

If She Can Find Joy

Chantal clawed her way out from the pile of bodies. She had witnessed the slaughter and had only survived because she was mistaken for dead. Terrified, but with a deep will to survive, she escaped to the mountains for refuge. Hidden in the dark forest, she had a perfect view of her entire village being burned to the ground. The air echoed with screams of the people she loved. She lived on grass until the killings stopped. Anyone found alive was savagely murdered. It was 1994 in Rwanda.

Unfortunately, she, along with her family and many villagers were Tutsis, the group being hunted by the Hutus. The Hutus massacred one million Tutsis in 100 days. Interestingly the Hutus and Tutsis coexisted peacefully for many years and shared many commonalities. Occupation by European nations, including Germany and Belgium, identified their minor differences.

*No one would blame Chantal for harboring anger for the rest of her life. In fact, they might even expect it. She speaks on her **decision** to live happily: "My family is living through me now. We were a happy family, and they always wanted the best for me."*

Who loses out if she remains miserable and holds resentment for the rest of her life? Correct, she does, and the perpetrators win. She doesn't condone what was done but recognizes being upset (or angry) for the rest of her life won't make it better. Spreading cheer is her way to heal and help others do the same— understanding the way to peace is not through a hateful heart, but through love.

Chantal now spreads cheer in honor of her people, those still living, and those who took their last breath in the genocide. Chantal says, "If I can smile and laugh despite all I have been through, can you? It's the laughter that has helped me get through."

*After her decision, she had to **believe** she could do this. Through practice **(action),** it got easier for her. Smiling and laughter are infectious. Chantal now speaks to large groups and shares her experience about how she was able to overcome the trauma of the atrocities done to her.*

The antidote to Hatred is NOT More Hatred, it is LOVE. The key to healing is forgiveness. As you do this, you can move on.

Build on Success

It's a simple enough concept— not always easy— but I believe in YOU. Do you believe in yourself? Practice this declaration to help.

My Declaration

Look at yourself in the mirror

Repeat as many times as you need to

"I believe in myself."

"I believe I can do anything I set my mind to."

"I will follow through and NOT give up."

"I will give it my all and do my BEST."

"At the end of the day, I can't control outcome, but I can control output!"

"I will put in 110% effort."

"I know if I do my part, I will have no regret and consider myself a winner!"

This is how one of the greatest basketball coaches, John Wooden, got the best out of his team! He told them, "I don't care what the scoreboard says if you did your best, you're a winner. Sometimes the other team gets lucky, or they may be stronger that day. But, if you didn't do your best (even if you win), you'll know it and always wonder." Do you see what happened here? The coach saw more than just winning basketball games. He cared about his players and wanted them to bring out the best in themselves; he got everyone to work together as a loving family, and the results he achieved were not only remarkable, but also profoundly meaningful.

Let's Get You In The Mood

It begins with posture, attitude, and your breath. Notice if you are slouched reading this, and if you have a critical look on your face, or if you are barely breathing. Are you sitting upright, breathing deeply, smiling, and in a state of feeling joy? If you are not sure, look in the mirror or at your camera (yes, use that selfie mode) and take a deep breath in.

What do you notice? Do your shoulders hunch up? Does your belly go in?

Sit upright, take another deep breath, and SMILE (yes even if you need to force it!)

Inspire

Breathing is our conduit to life. We can live for weeks without food, days without water, but many can only survive a few seconds without air. Breathing seems so obvious; we do it every day and don't have to think about it. Conscious breathing, however, is different.

Growing up in NYC, it seemed like everyone was in a hurry, and they had the *"go, go, go!"* mentality. Imagine taking time to pause, smile, smell the roses, and breathe mindfully. This could become a welcomed break. The great part is, it does not need to take up much time and can be done almost anywhere.

About Mindful Breathing

If your shoulders rose while you inhaled, you are not alone. I find many patients raise their shoulders and suck in their belly when I ask them to take a deep breath in, while I listen to their lungs. Although this may feel normal, human beings didn't begin breathing this way. As babies, we breathed from our abdomen— puffing the bellies out on the inhale (inflating them) and then emptying them on the long exhale (pausing in between each breath). Animals do this as well.

As we got older, we may have been taught to "suck it in." If you wear tight clothing, it can be hard to take a deep breath at all. My advice: *loosen up!*

Mindful Breathing Part 1

Sit up and stretch your body long.

Steady your gaze towards the horizon.

Imagine the crown of your head moving up and feel your head reaching towards the sky.

Smile and take FIVE slow, deep breaths.

Inhale, inflating the belly.

Exhale, emptying the belly.

** Keep your spine nice and long with your chest lifted the entire time. Shoulders should remain down and away from the ears, with the shoulder blades towards each other.

Martial arts, yoga, singing, and laughter emphasize the "belly breath." It brings a relaxing feeling when practiced (ridding our bodies of stale air and accessing the most oxygen-rich part of the lungs). It's physiological!

Still challenged?

If you are challenged to move your belly while breathing, try laughing. 'Ha ha,' it out on the exhale, and that makes it easier to inflate the belly on the next breath. You can even lie on your back with a book placed on your midriff. See if you can raise the book up as you inhale and lower it as you exhale. If initially, you feel a little lightheaded, know this goes away. It is just your body getting used to the extra oxygen.

If you haven't smiled in a long time, don't wait any longer. Start massaging one cheek and then raise it. Now the other side. Close your eyes and think of something wonderful in your life. *Yes, you are here. And YOU ARE A GIFT! You are precious. YOU ARE A MIRACLE. (Remember the SMILE Game earlier.)*

You may have wondered why I spent so much time on breathing. It's the essence of life, and the conscious breath allows us to BE PRESENT living life to its fullest. When life seems chaotic or out of control, I reset my internal thermostat through meditation. These deep breaths help me to calm down, regroup and remind me of what's important (ridding me of the trivial chatter), so I can move my life in the direction it needs to go.

Mindful Breathing Exercise Part II -
Now let's add a count:
Smile
Inhale for 4 seconds
Hold for 4 seconds
Exhale for 8 seconds
Pause for 4 seconds
This is one full breath. Can you repeat
this 5 times? Work up to doing this
twice a day. Notice how calm and
energized you feel with practice.

So what *is* power, really?

It's the ability to act. Nothing great gets done if you don't ACT. Though people like to believe in the adage that knowledge is power, in fact, it's not. I say this because I know plenty of intelligent people who are miserable. They know what they need to do to make themselves happy, yet they are not DOING those things. Coupling the corrective action with the right knowledge is key. If you don't, you may have the greatest intentions to see the sunset, but if you head east (where the sun rises), you will miss it!

I have never had a patient who *wanted* to feel terrible. Under the assumption you want happiness, we must DO what happy people do. You can't be sad when you're happy, just like you can't be stressed when you're calm. Simply put… To feel happy, you must ACT it. Laughter is the conduit.

Can you fake it until you make it with laughter? Dr. Kataria, the founder of Laughter Yoga, thinks so, and that's the premise of his program. He has people laugh on purpose, and with time, the participants note genuine laughter erupts. It's contagious!

It's the idea that motion creates emotion, a concept called facial (or neural) feedback. Fritz Strack, a German psychologist, confirmed these findings in his frequently cited 1988 research study.[14] He had subjects put a pen between their teeth (simulating a smile). The other group placed a pen above their top lip (simulating a frown). No explanation was given as to why they were doing this. They were then asked to rank the emotions of various cartoon characters. Those smiling had significantly more positive emotions compared to the latter.

Try it yourself. Move the corners of your mouth up, show some teeth, and think happy thoughts. Yes, ACT Happy. To some, this may sound weird, but what do you do when you don't feel good. Some may pop a pill. Here's a natural alternative. The act of smiling or laughing sends a signal to the brain that you must be feeling better, so it releases endorphins, and then *you actually do feel better.*

The same works for diminishing fear. If you ACT courageously with "Power Poses," for just two minutes a day, Princeton researcher Amy Cuddy found it can help you feel empowered.[15]

---

[14] *Data Colada*. Retrieved from (http://datacolada.org/wp-content/uploads/2014/03/Strack-et-al-1988-cartoons.pdf).
[15] Carney DR, Cuddy AJ, Yap AJ. "Power Posing: Brief Nonverbal Displays Affect Neuroendocrine Levels and Risk Tolerance - PubMed." Retrieved from (https://pubmed.ncbi.nlm.nih.gov/20855902/).

Your mind is powerful, and it takes cues from the body. That's part of the mind-body connection, and that's why conscious breathing is so important. It relaxes you and calms you down. This reminds me of the song from the 'King and I," *"Whenever I feel afraid, I hold my head erect and whistle a happy tune, so no one shall suspect I'm afraid. The result of this deception is very strange to tell. For when I fool the people I fear, I fool myself as well!"*

BAC (Behavioral Associative Conditioning) Method

BAC is a technique I developed to help you get healthier. Basically, you identify poor habits, disassociate from them, and replace them with options that serve you.

Because how likely are you to achieve a goal if you are too tired to even get out of bed?

BAC can help you improve your overall wellbeing—increasing your energy and making you more productive.

It teaches you habits that are serving so you can experience more happiness. As you get healthier, you tend to feel better, and you are more likely to ACT in your best interest!

As I mentioned, BAC is personalized and uses healthy substitutions to get you to your goal. We will begin to use it here, to set the stage for your laughter debut, which you can then build on.

What makes you happy?

1. Take 3-5 minutes to write down or record everything that makes you happy, including even the tiniest of things.

2. Cross out any items that are unhealthy or don't serve you (e.g., half a gallon of ice cream, street drugs, smoking)

3. Put a checkmark next to the inspiring items (e.g., playing your favorite song, spending time with good friends, going for a nice walk, playing the guitar, practicing yoga.)

4. Make it a point to DO at least one thing on your list daily to keep you inspired

Feel free to look at this list for a pick me up and add to it anytime you need to.

Did you do the assignment, or did you decide to put it off until later? Remember, an important part of the ACT habit is to do it NOW. It does matter! Because how are you ever going to get the BIG things done if you can't complete the small things? ☺

I don't have enough time

If you feel like you never have enough time, remember all of us get 24 hours every day. It is how we spend it that matters. Are you focused? Do you have clear-cut goals, and do you prioritize your tasks? I am not pointing fingers, because I will be the first to tell you, I sucked in this department. I wasted precious hours on trivial emails, social media, and watching TV for hours when I had more important things to do— like when I first attempted to write this book (several years back).

Take Responsibility

The past does not equal the future. Recognition is the first step. Denial never served me, and blaming others for all my problems just made me sad. So, here I am to repent and turn away from this way of being. I promise to learn from my mistakes. It doesn't mean I am perfect, I am not, but I am moving in the right direction. Step by step, I work to achieve my goals. Sure, I get sidetracked at times, but I have the big picture in mind and work to stay focused. If I fall off course, I just get back on track!

(**Side note game:** Reread the paragraph above, and read it out loud, so that "I" means YOU.)

I have heard from many patients, *"Dr. Gold, I am sooooo busy, I don't have TIME to get healthy."* So, I ask them, *"Do you have time NOT to (be healthy)?"*

Remember, every decision (or indecision) affects YOU. When you neglect your health, it can go away. Invest now or pay later. It is a lot easier to be on the prevention side as opposed to waiting until your body has less reserve and is weak and heavy (that's where my dad is at present), but I am proud of him for trying to get his health back on track by exercising regularly and eating better.

Statistics show the average American spends 4 hours per day watching TV. Then there is social media, texting, and of course, gabbing with friends and playing angry birds or candy crush. I'm not saying to not have fun (that's important). Just make sure to prioritize what you need to get done first, and then you can play. Managing your time properly takes discipline.

Focus and reduce distraction (even while you are reading this). For those with kids or taking care of sick parents, hire a sitter or recruit family or friends (or other agencies or groups) to help you. Consider outsourcing and bartering as you need too. I've hired someone to help me with emails and social media. It's worth it, I promise. When _you_ feel better, how does it make those around you feel? You are contagious, why not create something worth catching.

Back to BAC

BAC allows you to discover healthy substitutions, so you can reap the rewards. Let's say, for instance, you love ice-cream, but you don't want to experience the pitfalls of this heavy dessert. How about freezing bananas, putting them in a blender, and literally 'Going Bananas' with a new version of this one ingredient ice cream, (tasty and nutritious). ☺

Here are some other examples:

Junk food	**Uplifting Food**
Fries	Veggie chips
Burger	100% grass-fed/bean burger
Milkshake	Smoothie (whole fruit)
Ices/slushies	Popsicles (whole fruit)

BAC can be applied to many areas of life. One of my patients virtually smokes with cinnamon sticks. She visualizes them as her previous Virginia Slims cigarettes (a lot safer and less toxic).

Music Is A Gateway

Some say music is the gateway to our soul. Did you know this fact: lyrics are one of the last parts to be lost in a patient with memory loss? My great uncle, Hi, who suffered from dementia and Parkinson's, still remembered old songs and sang them with his wife (my sweet aunt Annie).

One patient with depression listened to sad songs that made her cry — not very useful when she was trying to feel better.

Create your own Playlist

Create an empowering playlist of songs that make you feel amazing! Here are some of mine: "On Top of the World," "The Best Day of My Life," "Happy," "Lucky," "Time for Me to Fly," "August's Rhapsody," "Inner Smile," "Can't Stop the Feeling," "Sugar," "Cheerleader," "All 'Cause of You," "Ain't No Mountain High Enough."

If you are having trouble getting started with the exercises, start listening to inspiring music. Start moving to get yourself in the right state of mind. Sometimes one needs to leave the house to get some fresh air and go somewhere fun. If you are experiencing any extreme or negative emotions that you don't feel you can overcome on your own, please seek professional help.

Speak UP

Here are a few quotes to consider...

(To paraphrase from the Bible) *As a person speaketh, so they become.* That is so true — you are who YOU say you are.

Ok, how about this one:

"Sticks and stones may break my bones, but words will never hurt me!" Hold on a minute — this has actually been proven to be WRONG! Words CAN hurt!

A powerful video on YouTube[16] takes viewers through several scientific experiments using words. From water turning to snowflakes, to rice and strawberries in containers, to plants in windows, each item was either spoken to with words or had a label on a notecard placed on its container.

Every single experience showed that the positive words had life-giving effects on the items they were speaking to, while the negative words had decaying effects on them. If this is what words do to items, imagine what they do to people!

How do you feel if someone curses you, pokes fun at you (remember grade school, unless you were the bully?), or chews you out at work? What about a stranger flipping you off in traffic? Gestures or words can hurt. However, when we recognize that it's not personal, but a reflection of the other person, (because in some cases they don't even know

---

[16] "You Will Never Speak Bad Words Again after Watching This! The Power of Words Are HUGE - YouTube." Retrieved from https://www.youtube.com/watch?v=MKy-DmnBdvI&t=14s

you), we can turn things around. To have an "extra" ordinary life, we need extra-ordinary psychology.

How we think — and this stems from our word choice — can determine the outcome of our lives. It's the law of attraction. You don't get what you need, but you get what you focus on. If you feel you will never get better, how likely is it that you will?

Words also affect our nervous system.[17] If you say you're in "excruciating pain," it can tense the body up even more and illicit emotions and feelings that are not conducive to healing. If you express sincerely, you're "in training to feel better," you likely will.

Here, we will begin to develop an empowering vocabulary (speak of what YOU WANT). I like to add fun to this because humor lightens the mood. As I mentioned earlier in this book, I used to suffer from a chronic painful eye and neck condition. In addition to treating this naturally, I decided to give my body ailments identities. I named my

---

[17] Kop, W. J., Synowski, S. J., Newell, M. E., Schmidt, L. A., Waldstein, S. R., & Fox, N. A. (2011). "Autonomic Nervous System Reactivity to Positive and Negative Mood Induction: The Role of Acute Psychological Responses and Frontal Electrocortical Activity." Retrieved from https://www.ncbi.nlm.nih.gov/pmc/articles/PMC3061260/

red-eye Sparkles, and my stubborn neck Charlene. I speak to them asking them "why are you here, what's the message?" Fortunately, I have been able to identify the problem and give them permission to go away.

I have sent them packing on a lovely cruise. They have been gone now for many years. When one of them tries to come back, I convince them how great a time they are having elsewhere. Instead of the condition rearing its ugly head, I am now able to keep it at bay and laugh with this silly story. It may seem strange to you, but as a medical professional, I am learning that this mental technique has merit.

The medical community doesn't know everything, and that's why we call ourselves practitioners. We play with many methods, looking for avenues to health with positive effects wherever we can find them. And listen, when it comes to pain, this sort of treatment is as inexpensive and fun as you can get. So, a prescription of silliness is JUST what this doctor is ordering. ☺

Until developing this technique, I often thought negatively and suffered for it. This lighthearted approach has changed my life. All of us have words that move and shake us a bit, making us feel chipper. It may be words we heard growing up or words from another country or our native tongue. It can be, *"Hey Mon, hang loose, No worries!"*

Terms of endearment, like 'honey' and 'sweetie,' come to mind when I think of my nieces. My coach calls her daughter 'Gracie Poo.' What words bring a smile to your face? These are words we can use on ourselves for encouragement instead of 'how could I be so stupid?' or 'what a bonehead move!' or 'I am such an idiot!'

Answer this… How Are You?

What's your response?

The typical answers are: *"Fine, okay, good. Not too bad. So-so. Can't complain."* What if you answered this question with such words as: *"spectacular, fantastic, unbelievable, great!"* When I said this to someone, they told me they don't want to lie. You are not lying if you **want** to feel this way. It is incredible how your mind works. Once you put out what you want, the brain searches for a way to attain it. Now it's YOUR TURN. PLAY the "How are you?" game. How many wonderful answers can you come up with?

When my husband taught this *game* in his classroom, one of his students challenged HIM to respond with "supercalifragilisticexpialidocious" (a delightful catchphrase from Mary Poppins) to the next person who asked him how he was, which was me. I 'pushed his buttons until he was furious' then asked him "how are you? Come on say it! Say it!" He said it and we both started cracking up. It only took one word to go from very angry to hysterically laughing.

My husband, the other Dr. Gold, is a business professor at Saint Leo University. He's a certified emotional intelligence trainer (a discipline that teaches people how to monitor their emotions). He's working on his own book on how to take emotional intelligence to the next level (through empowering people to become their own advocates).

Begin practicing how you want to feel. Using the inspiring answers you came up with, start responding to this simple question.

Notice how you feel. Rate it from 1-10. Give yourself a high 5 for making progress, (even by a point) and recognize YOU get to decide how you feel every moment!

Can you improve your score?

If you keep saying I am feeling fantastic, the brain gets

the message and goes there— if you are not there already!

"An EXTRAordinary life comes from an EXTRAordinary psychology. Otherwise, it's just ordinary." Dr. Tanya Gold, MD

Empowering Language Table

Here is a table I have created for you to start seeing the language people tend to use that keeps them depressed, oppressed, lacking hope and vitality (the Unserving column), as well as the language people who are happy use, to empower and grow (the Serving column). Which one do you tend to be in?

Unserving	Serving
Have to/must/need to	I get to
I feel terrible/lousy/It's a disaster	I have a hiccup/It's a bit disconcerting/It's bollocks

Unserving	Serving
I failed	It's feedback. I have an opportunity (for growth). What can I learn from this?
Can't/But	Can
Never	Will
I'm sad. I am in so much pain	I am in training to feel better.
I am terrible with names.	I am learning better strategies and will remember names. I will actually listen when I hear someone's name, repeat it, write it down, use it in 3 different sentences relating to that person & review it. I can even use humor, i.e., for the name Cherry, use her red hair as a reminder for a "Cherry on top.."

With these examples above, complete your own table of empowering language (can be on your phone). Continue to add to it, especially the cheeky phrases that have you glowing.

Do you speak what you want?

Have you ever noticed some people don't? They may speak in code as if certain people should know what they want. I used to ask my husband, "hey honey, would you like to stop for some ice cream." When he responded 'no thanks' and drove on, he couldn't understand WHY I got upset.

"Honey, I wanted ice cream!"

To which he responded, "So why didn't you just say that?"

Have you heard people say, *"I am not good at (fill in the blank)."* If you say that often enough, how likely is it that you will be? These statements can be harmful. They can keep people from even trying. What if they said I can get better at … with more practice.

My niece Mackenzie told me she's not good at math. Her mom apologized and said, *"You got that from me."* If Mac believes this, will she study as hard? How will she end up doing in the subject? Will she have any preconceived expectations? We must all be careful what we wish for.

Fortunately, Uncle Drew worked with her and helped her to realize she CAN do well. No one is accomplished unless they work at it.

Think of Michael Jordan, who didn't make the varsity basketball team when he first tried out in high school. His coach told him to train some more. What if he believed he wasn't good enough and didn't try again?

When I attended the basketball games at UNC-Chapel Hill, they were incredible because of all the great players. Did you know that Michael Jordan attended UNC as well as Vince Carter and Jerry Stackhouse? These players worked their butts off to be there and made the game look easy. We don't always think of all the effort they put forth, nor what they looked like in the beginning.

Jordan notes that he probably missed more shots than any other player, simply because he practiced so much. He wouldn't quit, and his misses just propelled him to work harder. Extremely gifted, he didn't rest on his laurels and continued to develop his skills to become a legend.

Simple Game: Speak UP

Take a moment and speak about the life you want using the _empowering vocabulary_ *you came up with earlier. What did you write in your eulogy? Did you commit to doing something (by stating in your eulogy that you DID it), or did you mention 'tried, maybe or should' in there? If you did the latter, please go back and change it now.*

How does it make you feel to honestly state, "I will do something," and then you do it?

The voices in and outside of our heads dictate our thoughts. They determine our focus or its lack thereof. When combined with an empowered emotional and physical state, the language we use can determine our behaviors. Here's my spiel: I can succeed and write this book. I am an author. I am happy because I create that emotion each day of my life.

It's a choice, and it is not always easy, but I know if I got up today, it would be another day to serve my patients, yoga students, friends & family, my kitties, and Drewie (my husband). It's an opportunity for me to write! I am living my purpose, and I love that I can manage my state and my time.

It's an honor to serve my readers and hope they can reap the same rewards from laughter as I have. It has surely rocked my world, and it keeps getting better and better! ☺ It doesn't mean you never have opposing thoughts. As I wrote this on the airplane back from Boston, part of me wanted to put on a movie. I already watched "Poms" (cute movie on senior (60+) cheerleaders), but I told myself one movie and back to writing.

I feel good as I am following through and not letting my subconscious dictate my actions, "Oh, come on. It's only one other movie. You can do work later!!!" Unfortunately for me, the deeper I plunge into my TV addiction, the harder it is for me to dig myself out. Besides, I would like to finally get this book done by this century (as my friends have echoed similar comments).

Ok, now it's your turn. Practice speaking about your life using the empowering language available to you. Take a deep breath. Smile. GO!

Review and take one action step to help you get closer to the goal. Having good health is critical!

Health IS Wealth (we will go deeper into this later)

When you have the energy you desire, you can do the things you want to do. People who mentally believe they can do things need a healthy body to help them get there. I mean, how productive can you be if you have trouble even getting out of bed? Thankfully, the mind is powerful and can help the body get in shape.

Edith, the 99-year-old powerlifter, suffers from COPD. She smoked for many years but realized if she didn't stop, she would die soon. She chose health and began exercising regularly. She didn't start powerlifting until she was 91. Her mindset and word choices are *"never give up."* Since she has been working out, her COPD (for the most part) has taken a back seat, and I see her pulling weights and lifting them with a big grin on her face! *"When I powerlift, I almost forget I have COPD,"* and her body has thanked her. *She uses an occasional inhaler and can walk without assistance.*

The great part is at any age the body can get stronger, both physically and mentally. This mental calisthenic reminds me of power posing.

** Power posing**

Amy Cuddy, a researcher at Princeton, found at least 2 minutes a day of standing upright in your favorite superhero pose can make you feel empowered. This is how I feel after powerlifting. It's boosted my confidence and ability to believe in myself.

The Power Pose Game

Go ahead and do a power pose for 2 minutes. How does this make you feel? Now take the 30-day challenge committing to do this daily for a month and let me know how you feel. It only takes 2 minutes. You can email me at "drgold@dgoli.com." Feel free to send me a picture of you in your power pose (G-rated photos only, please ☺).

Healthy Substitutions

Find healthy substitutions for the unhealthy or unhelpful behavioral patterns that you may have. For example, if you like crunchy potato chips, you can choose to go for chips with better oils or crunchy vegetables. If you are into binge-eating after a stressful day, replace the habit with going for a walk, calling a mentor, or joining WW or OA. Focus on your wellness. If you can't or don't want to reach out to a laughter hotline, watch funny videos on YouTube. Break your bad habits and replace them with good ones.

Psychology

Do you believe you can get better?

I believe change begins with our thoughts and the words we tell ourselves. You know the little choo choo train, that said "I think I can, I think I can…" I find this often to be true! What's more, laughter helps with this. Laughter can help shift your perspective on things so you can see things beyond you and find solutions to problems you earlier thought were irresolvable. Prolonged crying, stressing, worrying, becoming angry (basically any unserving emotion), on the other hand, does the opposite of laughter. It keeps you locked up and closed inside, so you are focused only on the problem and cannot look towards a solution.

I am not implying that sadness or getting upset doesn't serve a purpose. It does. It's a release and can be beneficial. The concern is to live there for long periods of time.

Use the principle of DBAC (Decide, Believe, Act, and Commit) discussed earlier to find the breakthrough you need. DBAC is a necessary ingredient to any success formula. Have faith and trust that things will work out. They usually do!

An important phrase for you to ponder: "To get well, you must believe you CAN."

Put another way, if you tell yourself you CAN'T ever get better, ever solve the problem, ever turn things around, how likely is it that you will?

Again, Your Language Matters

What do you tell yourself about getting healthy or getting older? I mention health as it pertains to seniors because they tend to be our sicker population, but these health principles apply to all age groups. Consider the following table and see how language affects your mindset.

Unserving	Serving
It's too hard (to get healthy)	There are many people who do it (get well), from all means: young and old, rich and poor, I will figure out a way!

Unserving	Serving
I can't do that *at my age*	Who says? Sister Madonna did Iron Man Triathlons in Hawaii in her late 80's, Edith Traina is a 99-year-old powerlifter, Johanna Quass 91-year-old gymnast and there are 93-year-old swing dancers and 100+ runners and cyclists. I'm NOT DEAD, so there is no need for me to act like it! I haven't kicked the bucket YET! I'm wise, mature, and these are my golden years. Even if you're dying (all of us are) so why not go out dancing. If you're frightened or scared, tell those feelings to "go take a hike, I'm going to enjoy what I have."
I can't do that (activity)	I CAN, and I need to do this, to stay strong and vibrant.
I'm too old for this sh*t	I am strong and getting stronger. I can build muscle and strengthen my bones at any age.

Unserving	Serving
I hurt all over (arthritis)	My body is speaking to me. I will respond by moving, knowing if it's arthritis, I will not damage anything. I can only make my body stronger as it will reduce my pain in the long run. I may consider pool or chair exercises if need be.
I don't have time (for my health).	All of us get 24 hours every day. There are many busy people who "make time to get healthy" because they know it's worth it.
It's too expensive	There are poor people who are healthy. Researchers have found it's cheaper than many think to eat healthy (only $1.50 more per day).[18] In addition, healthy food prescriptions could save $100 billion in health care costs.[19] I found being healthy results in fewer medical bills.

[18] Sifferlin, Alexandra. "Eating Healthy Is Cheaper than You Think | TIME.Com." Retrieved from https://healthland.time.com/2013/12/05/eating-healthy-is-cheaper-than-you-think/
[19] Settembre, Jeanette "How Prescribing Healthy Food Could Save Billions of Dollars in Health-Care Costs - MarketWatch." Retrieved from https://www.marketwatch.com/story/how-prescribing-healthy-food-could-save-billions-of-dollars-in-health-care-costs-2019-03-21

As the American College of Rheumatology puts it, *"Movement is KEY to LESS pain as one releases endorphins and becomes more fit."* Movement is Medicine!

Challenge Them, Don't Coddle Them

It's no easy chore to care for a loved one. It can be especially hard for us if we have aging and ailing parents to take care of. It is tougher because they took care of us when we were little, and we saw them strong and 'with it,' but now they may seem weak and frail, and appear to be moving in slow motion through a life that hurtles forward at a breakneck pace.

However, we have to challenge our aging parents if we want them to get well. How are we helping them if we coddle them (or try to do *everything* for them)? Especially with things they can do. So, when a child says to their parents, "Don't get up, mom I got this" or 'Don't do this; you will hurt yourself' as they try to lift something light, let me tell you it is a disservice to the parents.

The only thing such coddling achieves is keeping our parents *down*, and once that happens, you run the risk of making them stay there, instead of rising above the challenges that they are capable of doing. Let me share a personal example. I thought I was being helpful when I lifted things for my dad when he felt tired. However, once I did more research on the subject, I found several studies that showed how muscles only get stronger when they are used and challenged. It made perfect sense to me. I learned that a person, no matter how old or frail, can build muscle and bone at any age. That is why resistance training is so important! The seniors I train with taught me: "Strong is never wrong!"

The Power Gals

"What doesn't kill you makes you stronger"

These senior powerlifters (mostly in their 70's) range in age from 47 (yes, I am the baby) to 99 years young (Edith Traina) have shown that you can get stronger at any age. This sport is also safe — with no jarring or jumping— just a few second lift, fully supervised by the coach Bill Beekley, since only one person lifts at a time.

Fewer Injuries

At first, I thought that seniors should not be doing any powerlifting, because they will hurt themselves. That could not be further from the truth!

According to Bill, a senior powerlifter himself (and a powerlifter for over 40 years), *"Not doing it (strength training), is what causes harm!"* Because of a condition known as sarcopenia— where muscle is lost at a rate of 3-5% each decade beginning at age 30 (shortly followed by bone loss), you literally 'lose it, if you don't use it.'[20] Bill has been training these senior ladies for over seven years in Tampa, Florida. Under his guidance, he reports that no senior has ever suffered a direct injury.

It doesn't mean it's not possible, but these power gals have told me they got hurt from doing 'stupid things' having nothing to do with powerlifting, like swatting at a fly on one leg on a staircase without a banister. That's how Edith broke her wrist and she said, "Thank G-d, G-d is watching me!" Two other ladies got rear-ended from distracted drivers who

---

[20] Publishing, Harvard Health. n.d. "Preserve Your Muscle Mass." *Harvard Health*. Retrieved from https://www.health.harvard.edu/staying-healthy/preserve-your-muscle-mass

they suspect were texting (no broken bones). Thankfully all the ladies healed quickly, with their strong muscles likely contributing to the rapid recovery.

Benefits of Powerlifting for many of these ladies

- Stronger
- Less pain (neck, back, hip, knees, shoulders)
- Good posture
- Improved balance
- Builds confidence

The Power Gals

- Live independently
- Walk upright (no assistance)
- Many drive
- History of COPD, stroke, knee/hip/shoulder replacement

Trudy, 89, who had a stroke, notes: "I don't have time for that." She shows up to practice and does what she can. When a doctor told Trudy that she would not be able to powerlift after a shoulder replacement, she 'left him.' "At my age, I need to strength train." It all worked out well because guess what? Trudy is still powerlifting, and that's what she says, keeps her shoulder strong. The coach carefully monitors her progress and challenges her appropriately. Her body is responding, and she has been able to bench press more each day.

"This sport is just what the doctor ordered," Bill refers to me. The ladies train three times a week, squatting, bench pressing, and deadlifting. Most of the women were not athletes and began exercising with Bill for the first time in a long time, beginning with a tone and stretch class. Because of his background, he introduced them to weights, and it naturally evolved to lifting heavier and heavier as he saw them getting stronger.

The intensity of the lift allows the muscles and bones to be challenged more and thereby respond. "What doesn't kill you makes you stronger."

All sizes

I used to think of powerlifting for beefy guys, but Susan is a mere 94 lbs. Yet she can deadlift 115lbs. Her spaghetti arms have toned, and now she easily lifts what was once a heavy bag of dog food and a case of water – to the amazement of her family, herself, and the store clerk.

Who cares

"The older (& wiser) I get, the less I care what others think of me. That has made life more enjoyable!" -Bonnie

There is always a critic in the room; someone who will try to *stop* you from living your dreams or try to convince you that you cannot do something worthwhile. "You don't belong." Remember, those who care will want you to succeed and be happy, and those who don't, won't! Your allies *will* support you! Bonnie, 80, another powerlifter, does not even focus on age. "I feel great, and that's all that matters!" People have tried to bring her down or convince her she's too old to be doing what she's doing, but she just ignores them. What if aspiring up (getting older) meant just that — becoming wiser and feeling good!

All these powerful women have similar traits:

The Will to Live Their Dreams, Have Purpose and Meaning in Their Lives. They are Determined, Never Give Up, Show Up and Like to Have Fun!

I believe these are also the tools necessary for a supreme *quality of life*! I sum it up as the 3 P's: **Passion, Power & Pleasure**.

The Power Gals work, volunteer, travel, and some live alone. Edith recently returned from her granddaughter's wedding in New York City. They are also involved in other sports, including June who competed with the best in the world, in lawn bowling in California. Others play golf, tennis, pickleball, do water aerobics, and take part in a writing club and Shakespeare book club. Edith teaches line dancing, and even puts on a splendid variety show at her community theatre.

Play Time with the Power Gals

At practice, in between sets, we PLAY. Trudy likes practical jokes. The first time I had no idea why the ladies burst out laughing when I stuck my fanny out to deadlift. I was handprinted after Trudy innocently patted me on the tush with her bright white chalky hands.

We smile and laugh a lot, and sometimes we even dance and sing! We cheer each other on and support one another. This is one of the best teams I have ever had, and I consider

---

Reflection

What insights are you gaining? Are you making progress and challenging yourself? I BELIEVE in YOU and know YOU CAN DO THIS!

---

these ladies as the mom I didn't have a chance to know as an adult. My mother completed her life when I was 13. Monica, a reporter from the St. Pete Times, who did a story on Edith, told me, *"The ladies have adopted you, and consider you their daughter!"* That meant a lot. I have so much fun with them, I sometimes forget we are working out!

Shy and serious as a child. I'm on the left with my sister
Marissa & Mom

Our first year of racing. My dad, sister Marissa and me. I
am the taller one!

My 40th birthday party with my BIG Loving Family

Sibling reunion in DR with my beautiful family. Dad is in the bottom center

My Drewie and me 'Power Posing' in Jerusalem

My furry kids Bella & Prince

Edith Traina, 99-year-old powerlifter

Clowning around with the Power gals & coach Bill

Teaching a Laughter Yoga class

Habit #3— Ugly

"No matter how dark the night, light will follow"

-Tanya Gold, MD

This chapter is about various degrees of *ugliness* that hold you back from happiness. It may keep you from living your purpose and feeling good.

Debbie is my stepmom. We didn't always get along would be an understatement. As a teen, I told her, "I hate you and that you will never replace my mom!" As I got older, I appreciated her more. She's the youngest of five children and had a father who could get mean when he drank (I only knew him to be the sweetest grandpa). Debbie battled many storms including head trauma when she was young. Later in life, she had trouble focusing and finishing college, even though she could read a book in less than an hour. She also dealt with extreme mood swings and suffered from mental illness.

"It was a challenge to wake up each morning." The pressure only got worse with four kids and trying to get them to school and then herself ready. She was working to earn her degree and obtain her real estate license. For any parent, this would be a challenge, but add in the mental illness, it became a nightmare.

Her doctors recommended medication, but she received feedback that "you don't need that" and decided not to take the medicine. Her symptoms only worsened.

Each day became a struggle. The house got messier with old food lying around, and dishes and clothes piling up. It was hard to find anything. Chaotic. It reached a point where one time when I came home for a visit, Debbie looked homeless — wearing baggy dirty clothes. She appeared confused and burst into tears when I asked how she was.

Slowly, however, things turned around. With help, she began to get rid of the ugliness in her life, starting with the clutter. My sister and I filled many garbage bags with clothing that we immediately hauled to Goodwill (so she wouldn't miss them).

In addition, we spent the weekend making the house sparkle again. She continued the process after we left. Debbie also sought professional help and started taking her medications. With renewed focus, she became a community leader. When Hurricane Sandy hit her area, she was actively involved in getting people mattresses and coordinating services they needed, eventually receiving an award for her efforts. In addition to her home, Debbie cleaned up her health. She began exercising regularly and dropped her "muffin top." Moreover, she began growing her own vegetables in the backyard and looked into setting up a community garden to teach others to do the same. Her backyard now full of life gives her much joy. I told her about the laughter hotline, and she called in. She realizes that happiness is a choice she can choose to feel every day.

At present, she takes mission trips to Nigeria and has brought back some beautifully handcrafted, brightly colored clothing that she has given to the family. She's also traveled several times back to her hometown in Barbados to see relatives (which she hadn't done in years). A far cry from the past when I thought Debbie might need to be committed. Now when I see her, she is usually smiling and upbeat, letting me know about her next adventure.

You Don't Deserve That

Looking at Debbie, I can never say I know what people are going through. I can only speak from my own experience. I remember the time I was required to attend a domestic violence rally. The woman on the podium who I'll call Jane spoke eloquently about how she battled for years being beaten up by her husband. People wondered why she stayed and never called the police. Well, maybe because her husband was the chief of police. He threatened her and said, *"Who are you going to call? They're not going to help you."* Jane believed him because the other officers were his buddies. They would lose their job if they took action against their chief, or so Jane thought.

She felt trapped. He also promised to kill her if she left.

But something inside her told her she had to get away. Jane calculated and planned. Fortunately, with professional help, she was able to get in touch with other authorities and thankfully escape successfully from this tyrant.

When I heard her speaking, it had been over ten years since she left her abusive relationship. Jane rallied for women all over the world to give them hope and knowledge that they too could succeed in getting away, though the statistics may appear grim. She, however, tells women that are in similar situations: **"There is a way. Find it. YOU DESERVE TO BE HAPPY!"**

Finding Joy

Many things keep us from feeling joy. Life is messy. There's no denying there is ugliness in the world. People hating one another, being cruel to each other, man-made tragedies — just turn on the news. There are terror and natural disasters all around. But amidst all this despair, there is also joy and kindness.

There are teachers, health care professionals, service people, volunteers, dare I say politicians, and talk show hosts who are decent people! They care. They and many others are working hard each day to make this world a better place. Know even in the darkest of nights, daytime will arrive and bring in the sun. Other times, the moon will shine bright and light up the sky, so the stars can sparkle!

Growing up in NYC, everyone seemed to be in a hurry. It was uncommon to see strangers look at one another and say hello, let alone give each other a smile.

After 9/11, it felt as if a cloud had lifted from the city (after the smoke did). My sister told me how complete strangers would start up conversations with her. No longer were street vendors just trying to sell you something, but they would talk to you and share their stories. *The city turned nice."*

From any great tragedy, we can see people come together and start to care about one another. This also occurred after the Holocaust, and the genocides in Rwanda and Liberia.

Interestingly, the fighting caused by our tiny differences pales in comparison to our commonalities. We are all part of the human race, and our DNA is almost the same. All of us have heads above our shoulders and do our business from below (thank goodness ☺). We eat the same way, breathe the same, and all seek happiness in some form.

Has the World Lost its Sense of Humor?

If so, how do we get it back? Can it be as simple as appreciating one another and learning to laugh more! Hearty laughter connects people and helps them reach an understanding. It's hard to hurt someone you can laugh with.

Other Types of Ugliness
A. Limiting beliefs

What are limiting beliefs? They are the stories you tell yourself about why you are not achieving your goals. My dream was to open my own holistic medical practice. But…

"I am a woman. I don't have enough money or experience."

When I was young, I wasn't aware that women-owned businesses. I knew of no woman who did until I met Anne Hermann, MD, who started her own medical practice out of her home. She taught me how to do it on a budget and informed me that experience would come. Then, I met Martha Price, a family physician who had her own medical practice too. They set their own hours and were able to raise families while successfully running their own business (for many years now).

These role models became my mentors, and they shared their precious roadmaps with me.

For almost anything you want to do, there are likely others who have done it already (and if not, someone needs to be the first. Why not let it be you? ☺)

I am so glad for the guts, determination, and perseverance of our leaders. Some of my heroes are Elizabeth Blackwell (the 1st woman doctor), Golda Meir (the 1st woman prime minister of Israel), Gandhi and Martin Luther King Junior (who both stood up for racial injustice) and Mother Teresa (who helped the poor and brought the world's attention to it), Oprah (the 1st black woman to host a prime-time TV show and now influences millions on how to be the best version of you), Tony Robbins (inspiring us to live passionately), my Drewie (providing never-ending love, inspiration, encouragement, and support), and my dad (who created a loving family and always taught me to strive for excellence and follow through on my dreams. **Who are your heroes?**

These gutsy folks can come to you through their books, movies, YouTube videos, posts, or they may be standing right in front of you (the people in your life). Learning from them might be your fast pass— because they've done it. It doesn't mean we won't make mistakes, but there's no need to make all of them!

The Story

Create 2 columns: Old Story | New Story

Old Story: In the left column write down or record any reasons for not accomplishing your goals (or for not making progress). What do you tell others about the struggles you have faced and how it's kept you where you are?

What have you believed to be stuck, stagnate, unchangeable about yourself, because of your current or past situation? What might you be saying that is creating more of the same yuck, you don't want?

How do these beliefs serve you (e.g. do they keep you safe, protected, etc.)?

Are you afraid— scared of rejection, failure, discomfort, pity, feeling overwhelmed or fearful of success?

New Story— Now switch gears and put on your sunny spectacles. Rewrite your old story with what you can start doing? Let go of excuses or blame. How can you make progress and begin overcoming these challenges (no matter how small or big)? Remember getting help when you need it, is a sign of strength and if you are not good at something — outsource it! First know you can. There is a way.

Use past victories for motivation. What have you overcome? How have you grown and what did you learn? Who inspires you?

Once you learn from your mentors what to do, it's up to you to follow through. Let go of limiting beliefs that hold you back.

One of my patients didn't realize hers. She has four kids and thought she had to be "perfect mommy" and never take a day off (unless she was sick).

Whenever she got one of her terrible migraines, she got a mommy's day off, and her family took care of her. As you can imagine, she got these quite regularly and didn't understand why. Once we talked about taking regular spa days even for one hour a week, her spells diminished drastically. The last time I saw her, she couldn't remember her last headache. With fewer headaches, she's checking off items on her bucket list, having just completed her dream of hiking Mount Kilimanjaro and now the Pacific Coast Trail, (no longer having her headaches as an excuse.) Interestingly, she hiked the entire Appalachian trail with her girls and couldn't recall a single migraine.

All of us have a story to explain our life. If you have your dream life or are in progress of getting it, congrats and know there's no endpoint. Keep taking it to the next level. For those who haven't started or are not making progress, what's holding you back?

All of us have reasons (or excuses) for why we are not at goal. Be honest with yourself and let go of any 'truths' you gathered from childhood or the past that no longer serve you.

Know it's usually never the right time and you will likely NOT have everything you need to make your move. Do it anyway. Give it your best shot and continue to grow and learn. If I waited for circumstances to be perfect when I opened D'Goli (my business), I would still be waiting.

What if you started telling yourself "that it will work out and I can be happy NOW!"

The iceberg

It's a massive piece of floating ice with a large part of it submerged. The iceberg analogy teaches you that what lies below the surface affects what lies above it.[21] All of us have beliefs (whether conscious or unconscious) that can hold us back. Changing our limiting beliefs to empowering ones can rewrite our destiny. To accomplish, this, use some incantations like: "I am worthy of love," "I can make my dreams come true," "It's not too late to start," "I can go back to school," "I can take that trip," "I am smart," "I am enough," and "I can be happy."

B. Limiting people

Are there people in your life that bring you down? One of my old-time friends would call me to vent. Once she was done, she promptly ended the call and I felt lousy. I dreaded her call, but I would still answer because she was my friend.

---

[21] I also use the iceberg analogy earlier to explain the "extra" ordinary but doable work it takes to be happy (see illustration Chapter 1).

I realize friendship is a two-way street, and I sent her a letter explaining how I felt. She apologized and said she didn't realize what she was doing. She made changes, and it got better. Now our conversations are about us, not just her.

If people are bringing you down, it's time to speak up. If you find it difficult to say something, you can always send them a note, email, text, Facebook message, or even a Tweet (I am leaving out many other forms of communication because there are too many to list!)

Set healthy boundaries. In any relationship, ask yourself, *"Is this relationship good for me? If not, what can I do to make it so?"* It is important to know that not all friends have your best interests at heart. They may just agree with you while you vent and decide that life is unfair.

I agree life is NOT FAIR, but will that mentality get you to your goal or get you motivated to start or continue, plugging away at a big dream that will likely knock you down many times before you succeed?

Be careful of too many friends, telling you what you want to hear. Some of the BEST friendships include folks who are not afraid to give it to you straight — not afraid to hold you to a higher standard and not let you lie to yourself. They believe in you and are the ones who want you to be true to yourself and live to your full potential - encouraging you to look at your life with more truth.

Ultimately, they love the real you and want you to be happy, knowing that you can indeed cross all the finish lines in your life!

When you find the answers to your questions, take action! Do not delay it anymore. Seek expert counseling as necessary.

Abuse is also something to watch out for. People get used to being mistreated, physically or otherwise, and start to take it as normal. If the people in your life hurt you— for example, if they beat you up (mentally or physically), they are not serving you. Please seek safety and get professional help if you are being abused. No one deserves to live like that!

Here is the barometer: when you walk away from a person, do you feel uplifted, or uprooted... most times or do you feel drained, lousy, and degraded?

C. Distractions and Clutter

I did a home visit with a hoarder. She had clothes strewn everywhere, to the point you could not even enter one of her rooms because it was piled high from floor to ceiling with old t-shirts. She spoke of not having enough room and not being able to find things. She was also depressed because it was hard to get anything done.

A cluttered home can lead to a cluttered mind. It can also make it easy for you to lose things.

Simplify life by getting rid of the excess. You can give this great gift to yourself. If you have trouble 'letting go,' bring in a specialist to offer some guidance. I did, and it feels great now to have open spaces.

If you like to shop in excess, learn to stop, it will save you money!

D. Time Wasters

Go back to **The Time Log**. Where do you spend your time? Take an inventory. Spend one day logging this. When I did this, I found out I spent 6 hours a day checking inconsequential emails, social media, and taking calls from unknown numbers (mainly spam). Time is a precious commodity, we cannot get back, and I was wasting a large chunk of my day on trivial matters with little return.

Some advice from Timothy Ferris' book *The 4-Hour Workweek* is as follows:

- DON'T take calls from unknown numbers. Important callers will leave a voicemail, and you can decide when to return the calls.

- Have someone help you with emails. My intern took me off many lists, and I use a spam filter to help.

- DO protect the boundaries of your time. Focus. You may tell the caller, *"I am in the middle of something, and have 5 minutes,"* so they hopefully get right to the point.

- DO ask for help when you need it. Technology is not my forte, but I am getting better. I find the younger generation grew up with this stuff, and some techies like my husband, who builds computers, can do things quickly. If I cannot easily find the answer on Google, I ask one of them. I once asked my 16-year-old sister, Jaz, to help me set up my PayPal account.

She did it in a fraction of the time it took me just trying to figure it out!

- LIMIT TV: As Jim Rohn affirmed: *"Poor people have large TVs, successful people have large libraries"* Research shows the average American watches four hours of television a day. Coupling this with other timewasters, is it possible to free up some time to do the things that matter?

Do you procrastinate?

All of us do. According to Nir Eyal, a NYT bestselling author, who wrote "Indistractable," 'everything we do is to escape discomfort,' which can result in distraction and procrastination. To help counter this, use the "10-minute Rule."[22] First, be mindful of your time and practice "time boxing" (time calendar to get things done, i.e., 10-10:30 work on proposal 10:30-11 play video games. It's ok if you don't finish things. The important part is you stay focused

[22] Mindvalley. 2020. "How To Get Your Focus Back And Stop Procrastinating - Nir Eyal." *The Mindvalley Podcast With Vishen Lakhiani | Listen Now*. Retrieved from https://podcast.mindvalley.com/how-to-get-your-focus-back-and-stop-procrastinating-nir-eyal/

on the task without interruption. You can always allot more time the next go around.

If you do find yourself veering off course (wanting to do a nonscheduled task i.e. check the news or Facebook), *first take 10 minutes* to think about it or continue (or start) the task at hand for 10 minutes and then decide what to do.

More often than not, research shows by incorporating the 10-minute rule and time boxing, people are more likely to stay on track and get things done with less pressure.

"To do lists," as opposed to "time boxing," can be stressful, as they are typically lengthy, and many things DON'T get done. This trains us to be disappointed, as we are failing at achieving **all** our goals as planned. In contrast, with time boxing, if we stick with it, we are successful. I've tried it and I felt less guilty when I watched a movie, as I arranged it. Schedule in fun things to do each day. **Take charge of the day, or it will take charge of you!**

Busy, Busy, Busy

With more time-saving devices, people seem busier than ever. I see moms rushing around, telling me they don't have enough time. They have so much to do and can never seem to get it ALL done. Well, they can't! Trying to do everything generates frustration and stress and can make one feel overwhelmed. It is not conducive to living a satisfying life. Good time management is key to a happy life.

E. Word Choice– Yes, that again

From the time you started reading this book, have you been noticing the language you use daily? Are the words you express to yourself empowering, or do you berate yourself for being "such an idiot"? We can be our worst critic; we can be very harsh and judgmental toward ourselves without realizing the damage that it might do to us. It is important to understand that every experience is an opportunity for growth.

In writing this book, I encouraged myself with baby steps, that "each time I write, I am getting closer to my goal." It is easy to roll over in bed and say it is just another day, and I can do it tomorrow. But doing that would make everything optional— "someday I'll get to it" rather than today— putting your dreams on hold. I don't want that for myself or anyone else. Can you begin asking yourself each morning, "what is the MOST IMPORTANT thing that needs to get done today? and if possible do that first. Be fully focused and limit distractions. What will it cost you if you don't do this (if you make each day optional and don't prioritize your life)? The same applies to happiness. We must work for it and use our language for inspiration, not anguish.

Are Happy people just lucky?

When people see me smiling in my yoga class, they think I've always been this way. Not true. I work on cultivating joy every day. It doesn't come easy for me (definitely not natural), but it's gotten easier with practice. I've definitely had my share of tragedy. Many of my family members have completed their life early, while I was still young, including my mom, grandparents, uncles and aunts.

My mom died suddenly of a brain aneurysm at 40. My grandmother Doris developed Alzheimer's in her 60's, and it felt as if she was long gone before her actual demise. As you have learned so far in my story, my personal illness followed suit which threatened my vision, and caused me extreme pain — affecting my ability to work. But I don't focus on the hardship. I focus on the beautiful experiences they've given me. The short time I knew my grandfather, he used to play peek a boo with me with paper bags and had the cutest grin. Both my grandmas cooked me delicious meals from their native lands i.e. the best chicken noodle soup ever and curry goat with peas and rice. They gave me a lifetime of love and so did my mom. My mom loved the theatre and took me and my sister Marissa to see a show almost every weekend. She even started my friends and I, including my sister in a theatre troupe, performing fables to nursing homes, libraries and in the park — teaching us courage and learning when people laughed it was with us, not at us. After she died, my dad encouraged my sister and I to speak about the fun times we had with mom. He taught us we could still laugh, despite the sadness.

As for my illnesses, even these I am grateful for as they gave me a greater understanding of pain and what it means to be sick — feeling scared, alone and vulnerable. Thankfully this passed and I gained empathy with my patients. Now I realize I am NOT alone. Many people care, and G-d is also looking out for me. I am blessed to have so much love in my life. My Drewie, my kitties, patients, family, coaches, friends, and students remind me of this every day!

Love yourself

To truly love another person, you must first love yourself. I admit I didn't. It finally came through to me through self-reflection and not being so hard on myself— loving all of me, even my flaws. All of us have them, but now I focus on the good stuff and continue to improve my rough edges. This affirmation helped. Looking in the mirror I recite out loud, (as many times as I need to) *"I LOVE YOU, I Matter, I am Worthy, I am ENOUGH, and I AM Loved!"* It feels amazing!

If you keep telling yourself something (that is realistic and achievable), and you own it and believe it, it can manifest in your life. Now I feel the power of all those words!

Your Turn

What are the ways that you can increase your self-love and by extension, your self-confidence and happiness? Take action and include those acts in your daily life. Slowly, you will begin to love yourself— just the way that you deserve!

The "Undercover Ugly"

Our Subconscious Mind

Our true self wants to be happy. If you are not, you just need to retrace your steps and get back to that self. So what may have happened? How did you stray so far away from who you really are?

Learning a little about our subconscious mind might make sense of the trajectory that took us away from our true self and into 'the ugly'.

Your subconscious mind stores the thoughts that are filtered in from your conscious mind. Here is an interesting fact: you are not even aware of them. However, those thoughts that are hidden in your subconscious mind tend to affect your behavior and control your mood.

You can witness it the next time you find yourself upset, making some bonehead move like yelling at the traffic (your dog, kids or spouse), getting angry because your flight is delayed, your meal order came out wrong, or engaging in unhealthy behaviors like overeating, smoking, and having one too many drinks.

It is also true that these can stem from generations of programming. You may have been conditioned to respond this way, even though you may not even realize it.

For instance, I fully blame my dad for being late to places. He operated on 'island time.' Now I realize I can take responsibility and plan ahead to be on time in my own life (not plan to be late). All one needs is practice, and sure, we may screw up at times, but more importantly we learn and make progress. Now I am much better at being on time (due to my husband's influence. He learned from his father that it's about being respectful.) Interestingly, I have seen my dad and many of my siblings get better too, because the plane won't wait.

One takeaway for you to remember is to celebrate the victories, even the small ones! (This is a big deal for me because I didn't do this. I didn't want to appear cocky and I thought I needed to wait for others to praise me. Now I congratulate myself when I have done a good job (woo hoo I wrote 2 pages, I am on time, I watched 2 episodes of the Big Bang and turned the TV off, instead of getting seduced and watching it for hours.)

Are there people who limit you?

What about a parent telling their child, 'You are no good' and 'You will never amount to anything?'

These words are a mirror— usually reflective of what the guardian has endured. They may feel frustrated, have low self-esteem, which makes them use their offspring as a scapegoat. Again, this may come from years of conditioning (taught by their parents). Unfortunately, the vicious cycle continues. However, here's a fact: it doesn't have to. *You* can learn to break the cycle— if you have the awareness, the willingness and determination to do this.

Limiting Communication

Do your word choices tend to uplift you or bring you down? Do you frequently bitch about something, "seriously, where did these people learn to drive?" (or berate yourself "how could I be that stupid") or do you comment on what's going well? I'm fabulous! The quality of your life is determined by the quality of your thoughts which can stem from your words. Developing an empowering vocabulary helps. What you say about others is often a reflection about yourself? I am the first to admit I wasn't very kind. I had deep rooted self-esteem issues (low self-confidence and high need for significance.) I realize now that was the result of jealousy. I put others down to feel better about myself. Now I realize how silly that was and that we can all manifest greatness in our own ways. **No one is good at everything, but everyone is good at something!**

Insight

To keep our thoughts and words on track, we must recognize there's reasons for people's actions that we may not understand. If you witnessed someone cutting you off on the freeway, certain unsavory comments may come to mind. What if you then saw a pregnant woman in the front seat in obvious agony? What would your thoughts be now? We can't know it all and when someone acts erratic there's probably an explanation.

Speak it

What if we began choosing words that serve us (in essence speaking what we want)?

   a. There's probably a reason for why he cut me off. I hope he's ok. (Even if it's not true, it may make you feel better and doesn't raise your blood pressure!)

b. I *get to* go to work (or school) today versus *I have to* — implying choice and freedom.

c. This will be a great day. If I woke up on the wrong side of the bed, I'll just go back to bed and wake up on the **right** side!

d. I CAN lose weight. How might I do this?

e. I will make the time to walk 20 minutes a day for my health.

f. I am going to earn my degree.

g. I will take that trip.

The best part of all this is that no matter what you have been told in the past (to your conscious mind) you can train your thoughts for success. You can learn how to quiet the subconscious mind. Tell it "thank you for sharing, now shush up" if it gives you unserving thoughts, like "you're not smart enough," "you're not that coordinated," "you can't afford that," or "it's not for you." Now you'll say, "I am smart, I CAN and I WILL figure out a way."

How often have you trained your mind? We work out our muscles to strengthen them, so why not our brains? The more you practice something, the better you can become. Vanessa Williams and other great athletes can attest to this. The same is true for playing the piano, studying math, and playing video games. The more you DO something, the more you CAN DO it.

But what about teaching your brain to focus on what you want? This is something I wish I was taught in school. It may sound strange to some but try it out. *Good words, good thoughts, and good deeds*— encourages the father of Freddy Mercury in Bohemian Rhapsody.

What words do you tell yourself daily? Do you say to yourself, "This is going to be a great day" versus "I'm having *one* of those days?" Sure, unexpected things happen, but does that have to ruin your entire day? Do you have to focus on it? What if we added joy, meaning and purpose into our day? Let's create it.

> ## Have Fun
>
> What things do you like to do? (Make sure they're healthy and good for you).
>
> Write EVERYTHING that comes to mind.
>
> GO NOW!

Times up! What did you write down? Are you doing any of the things that you wrote (or all of them)? If yes, GREAT, keep it up and feel free to add even more things. There is no endpoint!

If you're NOT, what are you waiting for? Life is short and goes by quickly. Enjoy it. Choose one thing and start doing something fun each day. Here's something that has made a dramatic difference in my life— MUSIC.

The Tune Into Music Game

Music can change your mood in an instant.

Create an upbeat playlist of at least ten songs.

Listen to it when you first wake up. These songs can help you start your day in the right frame of mind.

While you listen to your playlist, I encourage you to start moving. Sleep can stiffen the body. It is now time for you to awaken it.

Move your hips and your head. Move your shoulders

Now, take three deep breaths in and out, as you move one shoulder back and then the other.

Smile and move the right side of your body and then the left, the backside, and then the front.

Stretch out your back, reach up up up up up up up, forward, to each side, gently back and REPEAT.

> Stretch 2-3 times a day
>
> (you will never regret it!).
>
> Stretching helps prevent injury. I've met many limber folks (of all ages) who stretch & feel great!
>
> Smile again.
>
> Bend forward while bending your knees (that will help take the pressure off the back).
>
> Close your eyes and just move in any direction that your body needs to. This is what I refer to as intuitive movement. Our bodies know what they need to do. Listen and tune in.
>
> *Be cautious if you get dizzy. Hydrate!

What Happened?

I have never had a patient who wanted to be miserable, but for those who are unhappy long-term, their programming may have taught them to reap the benefits of their behavior. It may have started early on when they scraped their knee and got babied, receiving more attention and affection when they were hurt or sick. This may have transpired into adulthood, seeking attention and love by appearing needy and this behavior may have been reinforced most of their lives (finding people to 'take care of' them). Sadly, if they only identify with this role of feeling helpless to control their situation, they may never develop the strength that comes with empowering themselves. Thankfully the #metoo movement has lent a voice to women who have been abused. This is not to belittle or make less of being a victim, but to simply note that living there for the rest of your life is not healthy. Victims may feel helpless to change, and without change, there is little opportunity for growth and improvement.

Some former high school heroes fall into a similar trap of becoming resistant to change. They continue to live their "glory days," telling their stories about the "big game," but they fail to move on and LIVE in the present. Have you ever seen Al Bundy on "*Married With Children*?" He was a high school quarterback who became a shoe salesman. In this hilarious sitcom, he's often plopped on the couch like Homer Simpson with his potbelly sticking out while watching TV and drinking beer. He bitches about almost everything, including his quirky family (but who doesn't have one of those).

A compelling future comes when you get *off the couch* and create it.

This is what Sarah did. After being sexually assaulted, she decided that this would never happen again, so she learned martial arts and began teaching self-defense to other women so they could better protect themselves. This dominated her life. One day one of her students asked her, *"So has this always been your passion?"*

"No, it was art," she remembered. *"It was always art."* At that point, Sarah realized that she sacrificed everything — including her life goal of being an artist– after this terrible event, but she didn't have to. Sarah returned to school to study painting, her true love. Yes, this horrible event happened, but she became stronger and didn't let it stop her from living her dreams.

FORGIVE

Terrible things happen that are not fair. You don't have to condone them, but giving yourself permission to forgive allows you to move on. Otherwise, you let the situation or person have power over you. In other words, set yourself free, so you can live your optimal life.

One sorry away

> ### The Forgiveness Declaration
>
> What is something you need to forgive?
>
> With emphasis repeat three times:
>
> "I forgive. I am choosing to move on and not let this hold me back any longer. I am DONE!" (Repeat as many times as you need until you feel yourself forgiving.)
>
> *Just recently, I forgave the doctors who misdiagnosed my mom. I can't even imagine how they must have felt. She died as a result.

I have met friends who haven't spoken to family members or friends in many years. One friend told me she couldn't even remember what it was about except that, "it was bad." In the heat of the moment, we can say things we don't mean. If that has happened, clear the air. You can't control the outcome, but you can control output. Consider the words, "I'm sorry if I upset you." This may be the beginning of a new relationship, or at least you know you did your part!

I recently had a spat with my own sister, but we worked things out after I thought about how much I love her. It took about a day for me to recover. And I can tell you, it felt great. Sometimes simple, precise, clear communication is all that is needed!

Thanks for sharing

How can you train your brain to be present, monitor your thoughts and teach yourself to **let it go** when a non-empowering message pops up?

For one thing, know that it's temporary. Just tell your brain, 'thank you for sharing.' Follow that up by saying, "Now pipe down, shush-up or STFU (shut the f*ck up)!" — Whatever works for you. You can even press a virtual cancel or delete button. Change the program, change the show, this is NOT my life anymore! Yoga and meditation help by keeping you present to observe the thought.

Turn it on

We get better as we do something more. This is a great skill to master as you learn there's no need to live inside of a disempowering thought. It's like watching a bad movie over and over again. Who does that? How many relive sad memories? I know I have. What if you flooded yourself instead with fond memories, leaving less room for the sad ones? Like a **light** switch, turn it on! Yes, it takes practice, but you can train your brain to push the buttons of joy over and over again. Focus on what you want, and your brain can take you there…Give energy to it! Ultimately it is your choice. This doesn't mean sad memories will never pop in, but you learn to make them temporary.

This may sound wishy-washy, but if something works, I'm in! Try it.

That's how great leaders operate. They have a vision. They can see it before it happens, and so it does. Who would have thought "the greatest place on earth" could be created from a swampland? That was most of Orlando, Florida, before Walt Disney's team developed the Magic Kingom.[23]

Have an inspiring image ready (i.e. holding your baby for the first time), so they pop up every time a nonserving thought comes into your head, then you will have some other

---

[23] Conradt, Stacy "Why Walt Disney Built a Theme Park on Swampland | Mental Floss." Retrieved from (https://www.mentalfloss.com/article/28174/why-walt-disney-built-theme-park-swampland

place to go. Remove the thoughts that break you down. They are only trying to stay rent-free, and they eat up your time and energy. Think of an uninvited guest. It's OK for you to ask them to leave and invite some fun people over.

State changers

Motion is a rapid way to feel better. Move. Get outside. But this is not always feasible. I used to go for a run, but if a disempowering thought comes over you when, for instance, you are in an airplane, that can be a little challenging. Know that you can go anywhere in your mind! You can also engage in some deep breathing, stretching, jam out to your favorite beat, and engage in a giggling session while recalling some fond memories. I also like to watch funny shows or look at videos or photos of my young nieces. Discover what healthy "happy state changers" work for you and have the discipline to do them. Review your happy list if you get stuck.

Be a kid again

As children— we laughed, played, sang, and colored. We were happy to be alive. We didn't analyze everything. True, we had fewer responsibilities, and as babies, we could nap, cry, gurgle, poop and spit up on people, and they would still love us. As we cultivate playfulness, we remember how good it felt to be young again. That's why I enjoy playing with toys, reading kid's books, and singing kid's songs! If you feel weird doing this or uncomfortable because you're a male hanging out at the playground or the kids' section of Barnes & Noble, ask a friend if you can babysit their kids. They will show you the way.

Other options include wearing shirts with cheerful sayings or pictures ("happy clothes"). Happy stickers with smiley faces can be strategically placed on your phone, bathroom mirror, fridge, dashboard, or computer and handed out to others to remind us all to rejoice more.

I carry smiley faced stickers with me everywhere and you should see the expression on people's faces when I hand them out. Priceless! Even with grown-ups! Adults can learn so much about being happy and having fun when we mimic a child's playful state! Just looking at a happy baby gurgling puts a big grin on my face. What about you?

Your Brain's Major Role

Your brain's main objective is not to make you happy, but to keep you alive and safe. That's why some folks tend to stay in the same rut. What they did yesterday didn't kill them, so why not just stay there for an indefinite period (like a dog chasing its tail, you will never get anywhere)? Have you seen the cartoon movie *The Croods*? They are cave people, and the earth is beginning to break apart. The father hides his family in a cave to keep them safe.

Then his spirited teen daughter ventures out and meets a cute boy, named Guy, who has 'advanced ideas.' Guy speaks of leaving the cave for higher ground where they can be safe long term. The father immediately vetoes the idea as too dangerous, but his daughter gently reminds him, "Dad, being stuck in this cave all day is NOT living. We are just *trying NOT to die!"*

While shunning yourself from the world may sound good in theory (you may feel protected and safe), it is just not conducive to a fruitful life. It's easy for one to become complacent, bored, frustrated, and scared to leave. You are doing the same thing day in and day out. Anything in life that doesn't grow dies. And the same applies to our dreams.

The less action we take towards achieving our goals, the less likely we are to reach them. Play to win (instead of playing not to lose.)

Most people who are successful will tell you it's not just the endpoint that was the most exciting part. It was the struggle, the overcoming, the determination to give it our all when everything seemed to go to pieces that made the culmination so sweet!

For me, it is like getting ready for a party with my sister. We have just as much fun getting ready as we do when we are in the midst of the event! There's no endpoint to success and enjoy the process. It's also important to take a break at times, so you don't burn out.

So, in order to *Tame the Ugly*, you need to spend some time training your brain to play nice. These next habits (the 3 G's) will help you along.

Habit #4 Give

"The Secret to Living Is Giving"

Giving is a meaningful way to forget your sorrows. It takes the focus away from you and your troubles and places it on helping another human being. Research shows it's also a great way to bring joy back into your heart.

When Bethany Hamilton lost her arm in a shark attack while surfing, she gave up the sport she loved completely. It was a mission trip to Thailand after the Tsunami disaster that surprisingly lifted her spirits.

She saw how much the people had suffered, losing their families and homes, basically everything. They were terrified to go back into the water, even though the coast had cleared.

Through focusing on helping a young boy and teaching him not to be afraid, she was able to get back in the water herself, and back on her surfboard. She realized then that no one could take away her joy except herself. Even with one arm, she competes professionally and has become a top athlete in the sport. Check out the movie, 'Unstoppable,' where you can see more about her current life. Bethany is an inspiration, and brings hope to others, showing the world that anything is possible!

One reporter asked her if she knew on the day of the accident, this would happen, would she still get in the water? Without hesitation, she responded, "yes."

"Without this incident, I would not have this much impact on others, as I do now." She realizes that she is not broken or maimed; she is just living her purpose!

The Heroes

"We make a living by what we get. We make a life by what we give."

Look at our service people— teachers, healthcare professionals, the military, firefighters, police officers, politicians (there are good ones), and so many others who sacrifice their lives, day in and day out, to make this world a better place. They fight for us. They show us there is a shining light at the end of the tunnel.

My brother in law was a teacher in the AVID program. It helps kids who need extra support to make it into college.

They are not brainiacs or mentally challenged. They are the children who fall through the cracks, the kids whose home life may be fragile (financial and/or emotional constraints), and they may not believe they can go to college as no one they know has done it before. They usually just need some extra help and encouragement in key classes.

In the program, they meet mentors, are tutored, and learn valuable skills so they can handle the work, and learn they can prevail. It's highly successful, and there are stories of kids making it into top-notch universities, including Harvard and Yale, and continuing on to graduate school.

How can you start giving more of yourself to others, if you don't do so already?

Many parents know how to do this quite well. Caring for a child completely dependent on you is a big sacrifice, although it comes with high rewards. It may not always feel that way, especially when they reach adolescence, but my sister's take on that is you don't want your kids so warm and cuddly then because it would be too hard to let them go! ☺

Giving Back

There are numerous volunteer opportunities in all capacities, including travel. Those at home can write letters and make phone calls. Even a simple smile can brighten someone's day. Remember the smiling game, and feel free to do it again. Can you beat your last score?

My siblings are some of the biggest givers I know. They learned this from my dad. He often fed the homeless and even employed some of them. He believed in helping someone whenever you could, my mom did too, not by just giving them stuff, but by teaching them to respect themselves and earn it. Often, we got windshields cleaned this way.

Now, it's our turn to have the honor to assist my dad. He's been diagnosed with Parkinson's but is adamant not to let it slow him down. He works out regularly with a trainer and has the best attitude I know — no complaints and smiles often. His lovely lady has suffered an osteoporotic fracture in her back and now has trouble breathing and walking, and is often in pain. It's not easy, but they help each other. Thankfully my brothers are nearby to do the shopping and help out with some of the household chores.

When you give from the heart, you get so much back in return (especially when you're appreciated.)

Fortunately, I've been blessed to meet some huge donors in this world. This includes Dr. Kataria (the founder of Laughter Yoga) and Patch Adams, a medical doctor who spreads cheer to millions by "clowning around."

As discussed earlier, Laughter Yoga teaches people to laugh on purpose to feel better. It's the way our body is naturally designed. That's why it feels so good. As you recall, this gift allowed me to overcome a painful illness by learning another way to behave (no need to be sad all the time, when I could ACT Happy). This laughter virus is contagious, and I'm fine with catching it!

Imagine being on a subway when someone starts cracking up. The nearby passengers may initially stare, but then they break out into a hint of a smile and then a chuckle. Without realizing it, you start to smile, and before you know it, your gut begins to jiggle, and YOU are full out hemming and hawing with tears streaming down your eyes, but you don't even know why! This gift is meant to be shared and a means by which we can bond in society, reducing stress and increasing playfulness, according to Dr. Kataria.

The real Patch (portrayed by Robin Williams in the movie, "Patch Adams") discovered that in his clown outfit, he too could bring joy to those around him. Even those suffering could learn to smile and laugh again.

In his latest movie "Clown Vets," a documentary on veterans literally on the brink of suicide, Patch is teaching them how to love life again by seriously clowning around! These veterans are now finding when they give back to others it helps them forget their troubles. Again, *it's hard to be sad when you're glad.* Patch organizes clown mission trips overseas for healthcare professionals (and now the vets can join in on the fun). He has everyone dress up in silly costumes and do some amusing things like get passengers at an airport to pose in a gigantic pair of underwear! It's comical and a wonderful gift to be able to laugh at yourself in a healthy way.

As a medical doctor, one of Patch Adams' missions is to build a medical center — to provide FREE, compassionate healthcare (which is already under construction in West Virginia at the Gesundheit Institute). This is where I had the pleasure of meeting him at one of his seminars. As a teaching center, he plans to show healthcare professionals how to be more compassionate when practicing medicine. His ultimate goal is to create a "well society" within the industry. Patch believes "medicine should be less of a business transaction and more of a human interaction."

Another jolly fellow I had the honor of meeting is psychologist Steve Wilson, "cheerman" of the World Laughter Tour. Interestingly, he arranged a full speaking tour for Dr. Kataria and his wife when they first came to the United States to introduce Laughter Yoga. Steve became enamored with this unique concept of intentional laughter after attending this giggling guru's laughter club in India. Like Dr. Kataria, Steve has positively affected many lives and believes in laughing for the health of it — "Good Hearted Living to Prevent Hardening of the Attitudes."

Receiving More In Return

Bella and Prince are my furry kids. They adore me, and the feelings are mutual. I sometimes drudge taking care of them (i.e., changing their litter and feeding them), but now I realize I am the highlight of their day! They look forward to me brushing and petting them as they readily jump up and purr loudly.

Give Back

I volunteer as a big sister with Big Brothers Big Sisters. It's a non-profit organization where you mentor an at-risk child and encourage them to finish high school and go on to college. It's fun playing with my little sister, Minnie. You let the inner child come out as you do the simple things in life, like going to the playground and coloring and drinking a cup of coffee. Yes, she convinced me to give her one (I added lots of milk). She said, *"My mom gives it to me all the time."* Her aunt confirmed this.

As for outings, I could take her to Busch Gardens or Disney, but that's not what the program is about. It's not about impressing kids with expensive items but impressing upon them that they are loved and that they matter. Mentoring from the heart. The mentors teach their mentees to believe in themselves and help them build confidence and do the right thing, so they can be better human beings and live to their potential. I have discovered that it really doesn't matter what Minnie and I do or where we go, we have a great time. We often laugh and enjoy each other's company. Giving to others without expectations and with appreciation is what leads to growth.

Habit #5— Growth

"If it doesn't grow, it dies."

It was always her dream to finish school. Forgoing her studies to raise a family, she vowed to return shortly. Well, life got in the way, and years passed. Still no degree. Finally, in her 90s, she realized it was now or never. Enrolling in the same college as her granddaughter, they both graduated together. It helps to have an ally, coach, or mentor to get you through. Nola Ochs went on to complete her master's degree at 98.

Another wise woman decided to top Nola's record. Doreetha Daniels, an African American woman is now the oldest person to graduate from college at 99 years of age.

"It's never too late to be what you might have been!" https://www.youtube.com/watch?v=i98lVo5qUoo

Are you growing UP in the direction you want to go to? In other words, based on your list of what excites you and your eulogy, are you living your purpose? If you did not complete this assignment earlier, please do it now. I'm your lovin' momma, and I'm watchin'! According to Forbes magazine, many Americans do not live their passions.[24] They settle. They are dissatisfied with their job, and that is where folks spend a lot of their time. Without a life filled with purpose, one may try to escape through TV or video games, otherwise known as "the living dead."

That, for many years, was me. I watched TV regularly for hours after work and then started the whole cycle all over again. There is nothing wrong with watching a show or playing a video game unless it takes over. Take for example the TV episode on the Big Bang Theory where Penny (the pretty blonde who lives next door) begins playing Warcraft nonstop.

It is an online fantasy game introduced by Sheldon (one of the main characters who is highly intelligent and particularly odd). She does exceptionally well in the game, and it helps her to escape feeling like a failure in her own life. The problem is it impedes her from getting important tasks done like working and maintaining general hygiene (to

---

[24]Bohanes, Michal. n.d. "'Following Your Passion' Is Dead - Here's What To Replace It With." *Forbes*. Retrieved November 9, 2020 (https://www.forbes.com/sites/michalbohanes/2018/07/05/following-your-passion-is-dead-heres-what-to-replace-it-with/).

the point she's living in dirty PJs and starts to smell).

Can you relate (hopefully not the smelly part, but with getting sidetracked)? Do you or someone you know spend hours on their cell phone, scrolling on social media, or binge-watching on Netflix or playing video games (maybe to the point that you lose track of time and wonder where the day went)? Do these activities eat up your time— keeping you from achieving meaningful goals? Do they affect your sleep — maybe because you stayed up too late? (Sleep is essential for recharging your body and providing you with good energy and clarity for the day.)

Whatever the case, as you recognize how to free up your time (under Habit 3), you can then devote it to developing yourself and have more time to do the things you desire.

[*On a personal note, I used the 12-step program from AA to help me overcome my TV addiction. Besides alcohol, AA can lend support to many compulsions.]

Live

When you are fully engaged in life, growth brings joy. It means doing something you love that is challenging, but not overwhelming! Stretch yourself and figure things out, especially when they're not going well. This may include doing things that are NOT always fun but will get you to your ultimate goal (like I'm doing now by rereading the manuscript several times to make sure it flows well.)

Turning Things Around

It was supposed to be the most powerful glue in the world. Instead, it was the weakest, peeling off easily, it couldn't hold anything together. Ready to give up and throw away years of research, Spencer Silver's colleague Arthur Fry brainstormed and asked, "What else can this be used for?" Have you heard of post-it notes?[25] I use them often, and in my opinion, it's one of the greatest inventions. I am so glad what was thought to be a failed design became an innovative creation. From anything that happens, one can learn, and something great can come from it!

A grief-stricken father asked what he could do when his young daughter was diagnosed with cancer. Now, Team in Training (TNT), his creation, raise millions in donations for

---

[25] Nick Skillicorn "The TRUE Story of Post-It Notes, and How They Almost Failed - Idea to Value." Retrieved from https://www.ideatovalue.com/insp/nickskillicorn/2017/04/true-story-post-notes-almost-failed/

cancer research and to help cancer patients afford their treatments. This money comes from generous donors and many new athletes fundraising while training to run their first marathon, half marathon, or triathlon. Many competitors race in honor of family or friends struck with this dreadful disease, but now one can even see cancer patients themselves competing with the mindset: "This will not defeat me!" Recently, the founder's daughter completed this milestone.

It's Not Too Late

At 65, he got his first social security check. *"I can't live on this. What am I going to do?"* He then thought, *"What am I good at?"* He had one mouthwatering recipe for fried chicken. He received rave reviews from his customers, but after the new interstate bypassed the exit to his restaurant, he was no longer able to stay in business. His town turned "sleepy" (if you watch the Disney movie *Cars*, you'll see it's about a similar experience).

He realized if he sold his recipe, he would just get that amount of money. To have sustained income, he needed to receive a percentage of the profits sold from each restaurant that sold his flavorful *finger lickin' good* chicken. He went door to door, asking businesses if they were interested under his terms. He received hundreds of No's. Finally, he got a Yes. Remember, if you ask enough people, someone will say yes. It's just statistics. Persistence pays off!

By the way, if you hadn't guessed it, he's Colonel Sanders, founder of KFC (Kentucky Fried Chicken). How many restaurants are there now that use his recipe? ☺

I once asked to speak at a large firm. They said no. I didn't let that stop me and went back the next year. They gave me the same answer. The third time was the charm. This time, they welcomed me as their keynote speaker, and I was able to speak at their event to 200 employees on the "Benefits of Laughter."

Nobel

What do you think of when you hear the word 'Nobel?' Probably the Nobel Peace Prize. Back in his day, the founder of the prize Alfred Nobel wasn't known for that. This became clear when his brother died, and the newspapers mistakenly wrote about him instead. Known as the inventor of guns that killed thousands of people, he made a fortune.

He didn't want to go down in history as a murderer, however. Instead, he thought about what good he could do with all this money. He invested it intelligently for many years, and because of his long-term plans, his estate is still able to finance generous awards each year to those promoting peace in this world or making profound contributions to the sciences, years after he died.

Habit #6— Gratitude

"When I started counting my blessings, my whole world turned around"

-Willie Nelson

Gratitude is focusing on what you Do Have, rather than on what you don't. It begins with self-love, knowing that you are enough, you are worthy, and that you matter. Love yourself so you can love others and appreciate what you do have.

One of my friends, Edith, fits this bill to a T. She is grateful for just being alive. At 99, can you blame her?

"Every day above ground is a great day! Life is short; why not enjoy it!" To boot, she powerlifts. Yep, she lifts heavy weights. beginning this sport at age 91, after she was diagnosed with COPD as mentioned earlier. She smoked heavily. Not one to dwell in pity parties, she knew if she didn't shape up, she would ship out, as she was becoming short of breath just sitting in her recliner watching TV.

I've never heard Edith *kvetch* (complain) about anything, and she hasn't had it easy. She doesn't dwell on the pain or difficulties in her life. "Why waste your energy on negativity, it just drains you? I rather focus on what's going well. It feels a heck of a lot better! If I have nothing nice to say, I don't say *anything at all.*"

Let me give you a bit of her backstory. Her spouse was diagnosed with polio in his early 30s. After which, she had to raise five kids by herself, including caring for her sick husband and figure out a way to pay the bills. Prior to this, she was a housewife, as many were in the 1950s. She worked three jobs in the garment district in New York City to support her family, refusing to rely on government assistance.

"I didn't have time to be tired. I am blessed that G-d looks after me."

Edith is part of that group I introduced you to in chapter 2, known as the "Power Gals" (Senior Powerlifters), part of Tampa Bay Stronglife coached by Bill Beekley and Tony Conyers at Crossfit Jaguar. These gals, like Edith, appreciate their lives, reaping the rewards through their dedication and hard work.

Common characteristics of the Power Gals:

1. Live independently
2. Walk upright (without assistance)
3. Drive
4. Feel stronger
5. More confident
6. Reduced pain in their back, neck, hip, and shoulder
7. Improved bone density
8. Many of the women are over 75 years old

In contrast to what I learned growing up, getting older doesn't necessarily equate to "falling apart." It can mean gaining wisdom and appreciation of your changing body - working with it to keep it as healthy as possible for as long as possible. It's not too late (or too early) to begin.

The whole team reminds me of how blessed I am to be a part of their group. They've adopted me as their daughter, and I feel I have many moms now (as my own left early).

Would you believe no one has gotten injured directly from this practice, and we've been doing it for almost seven years? (Only one person lifts at a time and Bill, the coach watches closely to make sure they exhibit proper form.)

This speaks highly of Bill, as these ladies are at high risk for injuries simply because of the sheer number of ailments they already had prior to lifting including:

*Torn rotator cuff

*Stroke

*COPD

*Back pain

*Arthritic knees

*Osteoporosis

*Breast Cancer

Count your blessings

Some people may get consumed with their woes and forget what they have going for them. They may take for granted their ability to see or hear or get up in the morning, or that their heart is still beating, their lungs are working, and they have arms, legs, fingers, and toes.

An amputee once told me she would "love to have knee pain," because that meant she had a knee. Remember all the things going well— big and small— and think of the folks who love you. The more you appreciate what you have, the more meaningful life becomes. This is what breeds happiness.

Instill Self-Love Daily ♥

Look into your eyes & say this with love:

I Love YOU

I Matter

I am Worthy

I am Enough

Repeat as many times as you need.

Take the 30-day Gratitude challenge. Write down at least three new things each day that you are thankful for. I put my list into a "Blessing Jar" that I can look at any time and continue to add to.

A Superhero

He will live, but it does not look good. Rich, famous, active, handsome, and kind, this charismatic man seemed to have it all. In preparation for the cross-country portion of an equestrian event in Culpepper, Virginia, he went out for a practice ride. Two jumps, no problem. Prior to his third jump over a zig-zag shaped fence, his horse, Eastern Express, stopped dead in his tracks. The momentum and fast pace had him fly off the horse headfirst and into a rail. He was unable to brace himself, as his hands got tangled up in the bridle and the reins.

The next thing he remembers is being told he was paralyzed from the neck down and had a tube to breathe for him. Of course, he was devastated. He even contemplated suicide. In his autobiography, 'Still Me,' he wrote that he suggested early on to his wife, 'Maybe we should let me go.' She responded, 'I'll be with you for the long haul, no matter what. You're still you, and I love you.'
Those were 'the words that saved my life.'

With that encouragement, he decided to focus on what is still good in this world and he survived.

Even in his formidable chair with a tube dangling from his neck, he showed the world his adorable boyish grin, his signature smile that made Lois Lane's heart melt as well as mine. He was Christopher Reeve, popularly known as 'Superman.' He *played* a superhero, but became one in real life!

How he and his wife Dana handled his accident became an inspiration. Having good health is one of those gifts, that's not always appreciated until it's gone.

Habit #7— Health

"If I knew I'd live this long, I would have taken better care of myself!"

-Mickey Mantle

Folks are living longer than ever. This is definitely a miracle when you think of how some people drive! Thank goodness for smart cars. In America today, the average woman will live to 87 and the average man to 84 (if they haven't suffered from cancer or heart disease). In contrast to the 1900s, when a person lived to just 49 years old.[26]

Your health matters!

I don't know anything more important than YOU! Good health feeds vitality, making you feel better, and making it easier to be happy. This chapter will take a common sense approach (CSA) to valuing your health and realizing the time to focus on it is NOW. If you're doing that already, good for you and know there's no endpoint to how strong or healthy

---

[26] Leonhardt, David "Life Expectancy Data - The New York Times." Retrieved from https://www.nytimes.com/2006/09/27/business/27leonhardt_sidebar.html

you can become. The same goes for happiness! If you're not close to any of this or you're still on a bumpy road, know there is hope! Your body is meant to heal. Improvement, no matter how small, is still an improvement. As I remarked before, every victory is a VICTORY!

Going through the other chapters, including the exercises, will help remove many barriers to gaining health. I am glad this is the final habit, as it is the culmination of all the others. When you live your purpose, when you act, get rid of the garbage (ugliness) of life and any limiting beliefs or self sabotagers and start giving, growing, and appreciating all your gifts— your life takes on a whole new dimension.

Combine this with consuming REAL food (and beverages) with fewer preservatives, regular activity (including weights), and good stress management skills— this is the recipe for an optimal life — one that leaves you feeling fulfilled. Remember, this practice is a marathon, not a sprint, and consistency of these good habits (while not always sexy) allows you to have the energy you desire to do the things you love. Health and happiness feed each other. This can make you UNSTOPPABLE. As you engage in these enriching habits, you might notice that you need to get out of your comfort zone and engage with others, which is also beneficial. As you become healthier, you can *sail* through life, rather than feel anchored to a sinking ship!

The Wonders of Modern Medicine

Deadly diseases such as blood clots and major infections, including HIV (which has now become more of a chronic disease) are now treatable. It's miraculous really when I think of how Western medicine can transplant organs, replace or reattach limbs (like my niece's pinky), and repair joints (like the many bionic parts of my mother-in-law — both hips and knees have been replaced.)

Even burns can be treated with spray-on skin cells (as if one's painting a car.) Vaccinations have virtually eradicated some diseases (i.e., smallpox, polio) that decimated and crippled populations. Modern medicine, combined with improved working conditions and better sanitation, has contributed to these beneficial outcomes. There's no question many medicines work, but do they make the body stronger, treat the underlying root cause of the disease, and build the immune system? Not usually.

Many people on meds are living longer than ever **with** their chronic diseases.

But the BIG question is: *How are they living?*

*Warning the next few sections may be a little distressing, but it gets happier I promise! ☺

US Health Facts

- Nearly 70% of Americans take at least one prescription drug, more than half take two.[27]

- 19% of children are on at least one prescription drug.[28]

- 68% of seniors 65+ are disabled and have cognitive impairment.[29]

- Thirteen million individuals live in paid long-term care facilities (63% seniors, 37% younger than that,

---

[27] "Nearly 7 in 10 Americans Take Prescription Drugs, Mayo Clinic, Olmsted Medical Center Find." *Https://Newsnetwork.Mayoclinic.Org/.* Retrieved from https://newsnetwork.mayoclinic.org/discussion/nearly-7-in-10-americans-take-prescription-drugs-mayo-clinic-olmsted-medical-center-find/

[28] Dima M. Qato, G. Caleb Alexander, Jenny S. Guadamuz and Stacy Tessler Lindau "Prescription Medication Use Among Children and Adolescents in the United States | American Academy of Pediatrics." Retrieved from https://pediatrics.aappublications.org/content/142/3/e20181042

[29] *Friedland Robert B., Ph.D.* Selected Long-Term Care Statistics | Family Caregiver Alliance." Retrieved from https://www.caregiver.org/selected-long-term-care-statistics

who are unable to care for themselves).[30]

- 40 million suffer from anxiety.[31]

- 16 million adults suffer from major depression.[32]

- More than one-third of US citizens are obese (the majority are overweight).[33]

- Chronic disease plagues many, and it is driven primarily by poor lifestyle.[34]

- Heart disease is the leading cause of death with cancer not far behind.

- **$365,000,000,000,000** (3.65 Trillion) spent on health care costs in 2018 (17.9% of the US GDP) and the price keeps soaring (it was 12.9 billion in 1950). [35]

- WHO ranked the US 37th in healthcare (dead last

---

[30] *Friedland Robert B., Ph.D..* "Selected Long-Term Care Statistics | Family Caregiver Alliance." Retrieved from https://www.caregiver.org/selected-long-term-care-statistics

[31] Anxiety Disorders: Types, Causes, Symptoms & Treatments." Retrieved from https://my.clevelandclinic.org/health/diseases/9536-anxiety-disorders

[32]"Facts & Statistics | Anxiety and Depression Association of America, ADAA." https://adaa.org/about-adaa/press-room/facts-statistics

[33]Overweight & Obesity Statistics | NIDDK." *National Institute of Diabetes and Digestive* https://www.niddk.nih.gov/health-information/health-statistics/overweight-obesity

[34] "About Chronic Diseases | CDC." Retrieved from https://www.cdc.gov/chronicdisease/about/index.htm

[35] *Friedland Robert B., Ph.D..* "Selected Long-Term Care Statistics | Family Caregiver Alliance." Retrieved from https://www.caregiver.org/selected-long-term-care-statistics

compared with other industrialized nations).[36]

- The 2015-2017 Commonwealth Fund report showed:[37]

— "The U.S. ranked in last place among the 11 countries for health outcomes, equity, and quality, despite having the highest per capita health earnings.

—The U.S. also had the highest rate of mortality amenable to healthcare, meaning more Americans die from poor care quality than any other country involved in the study.

—Poor access to primary care in the U.S. has contributed to inadequate chronic disease prevention and management, delayed diagnoses, and safety concerns, among other issues."

What the heck is going on?

Fast Food Nation

1. We live in a culture where it's common to live

---

[36] Tanne, Janice. 2006. "US Gets Mediocre Results despite High Spending on Health Care." *BMJ : British Medical Journal* 333(7570):672.https://www.ncbi.nlm.nih.gov/pmc/articles/PMC1584360/
[37] Harrison Cook "Among 11 Countries, US Ranks Last for Health Outcomes, Equity and Quality." Retrieved from (https://www.beckershospitalreview.com/quality/among-11-countries-us-ranks-last-for-health-outcomes-equity-and-quality.html)

unwell. More than one in three American adults (and children) consume fast food on any given day. It's **SAD** ☹ (literally known as the Standard American Diet).[38]

2. One in ten adults consumes fresh fruits and vegetables.[39] Nine in ten children didn't get enough vegetables. American toddlers were more likely to eat french fries than green vegetables.[40]

3. One in three children is physically active every day (but less than 5% of adults are). Only 1 in 3 adults are getting enough exercise per week.[41]

The Problem

I know it may seem obvious to want health and do everything to have it, but in our society, most Americans

---

[38] Brett Molina. "More than 1 in 3 Americans Eat Fast Food in a given Day, CDC Finds." Retrieved from https://www.usatoday.com/story/news/nation-now/2018/10/03/americans-eat-fast-food-daily-cdc-survey/1507702002/.
[39] 2016. "CDC Press Releases." *CDC*. Retrieved from https://www.cdc.gov/media/releases/2017/p1116-fruit-vegetable-consumption.html).
[40] Dennis Thomps "Many U.S. Children Go Days without Eating Any Vegetables, Survey Finds." Retrieved from https://www.cbsnews.com/news/children-not-eating-vegetables-survey/)
[41] President's Council on Sports, Fitness &. Nutrition. 2012. "Facts & Statistics." *HHS.Gov*. Retrieved from https://www.hhs.gov/fitness/resource-center/facts-and-statistics/index.html

don't live a healthy lifestyle. One study in the Huffington Post showed less than 9% of Americans engaged in all four healthy lifestyles. Those who do work out, may not eat healthy, or engage in unhealthy behaviors, i.e., smoking, excess drinking, or taking street drugs. Those who eat healthy may obsess about it. People may not get adequate rest. It's about caring for your entire body.

I have met Americans who spend more time researching a vacation, or researching buying a car or home, than on their own health. How often do you meal plan or schedule your workouts, and then follow through?

Our culture is also about getting what we want when we want it. Immediate gratification predominates.

Like Fiona in Charlie and the Chocolate Factory whines, "I want it NOW." Fast food restaurants are in abundance (in the US, there were over 247,000 in 2018).[42] Folks flock to them because they're convenient, affordable, and many people find the food appealing. In addition, with the internet,

---

[42] Christof Baron, "Establishments in the U.S. Fast Food Industry 2018 | Statista." Retrieved from https://www.statista.com/statistics/196619/total-number-of-fast-food-restaurants-in-the-us-since-2002/

one can order almost anything from a pizza to a beer and get it right away. Western medicine feeds this mentality. It's entrenched in treating symptoms, with little emphasis on prevention and wellness, or treating the root cause. Outside of a physical exam, I was taught to have patients come in when they're sick (often waiting 'til they feel bad to make an appointment). Even with my own doctor, there are few opportunities for well visits under our insurance plan.

When patients come in, they want to be "fixed" with a prescription. One time my sister asked me for a Tylenol. Why? Because I have a headache. Why do you have a headache? Because I'm dehydrated.

Thankfully this is changing where I am finding more folks interested in well care rather just sick care. They want to prevent illness and keep their immune system strong, rather than just treat symptoms.

Ted came in for two days of a runny nose and low-grade fever. He took Ibuprofen (sick care) for the fever. After our discussion, he recognized that a low-grade fever was his body's natural way to kill the virus, and learned that Ibuprofen could actually block the healing process and mask symptoms. A better option would be some vitamin C to boost his immune system (well care) along with rest and fluids. Interestingly, in medical school, I never studied one healthy patient (only sick ones). Can you imagine investigating poor people to learn how to be rich? It seems backward.

However, our society wasn't always this way. We used to eat real food, exercised regularly, and generally rode out a simple cold on our own. How did our mentality change (from wellness to sickness)? Let's go back in history for some clues.

The Junk Food Timeline

The 1790s— Over 95% of Americans lived on rural farms.[43] They had an intimate connection with the land. Since people grew their own food, they knew exactly where it came from. Nothing processed, just food in its purest, unadulterated form as our Creator intended. Once picked, they ate it fresh. Fitness guru Jack Lalanne said it best, "If G-d made it, I'll eat it!"

---

[43] "Population & Food: Facts and Trivia." Retrieved from http://www.foodreference.com/html/f-population-trivia.html

The 1840s— The Industrial Revolution. This was a time of great progress. Machines were created that could do things faster and more efficiently than man (or woman) alone, i.e., steam engines, factory lines, automation, etc. Now, they needed operators. People moved away from their farms, to these businesses for steady pay and a better life. As more people lived closer together, these densely populated areas blossomed into towns, and then grew into big cities. Since fewer people grew their own food, they were now reliant on outside sources, and hence they began to distance themselves from the land, and where their food came from. Less than 40% of the population in 1900 had a farm.[44,45]

The 1900s — Pure to Processed: Creating Food to Last

Industries capitalized on this growing need. They produced chemicals and preservatives that were added to food to extend its shelf life. Hence the age of 'processed foods' was created. Nathan's hotdogs were one of the

[44]"The Evolution of American Agriculture — Jayson Lusk." Retrieved from http://jaysonlusk.com/blog/2016/6/26/the-evolution-of-american-agriculture

[45]July 16, Updated, Changes In Urban/Rural U.S. Population." *SeniorLiving.Org*. Retrieved from https://www.seniorliving.org/history/1800-1990-changes-urbanrural-us-population/

earliest creations available in 1910, and so was SPAM (processed meat in a box). In 1921, the first fast food restaurant was established— there was White Castle, then Wendy's, and then McDonald's in 1948. The growth of factories and chemical plants brought more pollution leading to a host of illnesses, including asthma.[46]

Tracking your food

As food traveled further from the source, it became harder and harder to find out exactly where your fruits, vegetables, dairy, eggs, and meat came from, unless you purchased it from a local farm.

At the supermarket, it says the country or state, but finding out which specific farm, when it was picked, or slaughtered is almost impossible. I tried to get this information once from a Whole Foods manager, and he just looked at me like I had three eyeballs! I prefer buying this from local markets for this very reason. In addition, the food tends to be fresher and, in my opinion, tastes better.

---

[46]US EPA, OAR. 2015. "Progress Cleaning the Air and Improving People's Health." *US EPA*. Retrieved from https://www.epa.gov/clean-air-act-overview/progress-cleaning-air-and-improving-peoples-health

The Solution

Many leading experts have characterized US healthcare as a crisis due to exorbitant costs, problems with access, and rampant chronic disease.[47] What if we applied a novel approach to solving this dilemma?

The George Costanza Principle

Let me explain. In the hit TV show Seinfeld, George tells Jerry, "I've been doing it wrong all these years. Every decision I have ever made has been wrong." "Well," Jerry replies, "if all your instincts have been wrong, then doing the opposite would be right!" George agrees, so he starts doing "the opposite" of what he would normally do, and his whole world turns around.

He begins dating a beautiful woman. She agrees to go out with him after he spouts out with confidence that he is "unemployed and lives with his parents." He gets the job of his dreams, after he yells at George Steinbrenner (manager of the NY Yankees), to finally do something inspiring with his team, instead of letting his ego get in the way. With a job,

---

[47] "Half A Century Of The Health Care Crisis (And Still Going Strong)." Retrieved from
https://www.healthaffairs.org/do/10.1377/hblog20180904.457305/full/

he could finally move out of his parent's home!

In an interview after this episode, George notes he met several guys who have been implementing this method with good results. Is there some truth? It's similar to Einstein's definition of insanity: doing the same thing over and over and expecting a different result. One needs to do something differently in order to get change.

What if we applied 'the George principle' to healthcare? (Do the opposite)

Now	**Instead**
Spend A LOT	Spend LESS
Eat junk food	Eat REAL Food
Treat symptoms	Treat the Cause
Prescriptions	Herbs (evidence-based)
Wait for illness	Prevent it

What if we spent less and got more? Sounds ironic but it's actually possible.

Preventing Illness

"What makes more sense: waiting for an illness to occur or preventing it in the first place?"

Trust for America's Health has estimated that an investment of only $10 per person per year in community-based programs tackling physical inactivity, poor nutrition, and smoking could yield more than $16 billion in medical cost savings annually within five years.

 This savings represents an annual return of $5.60 on each dollar spent, without considering additional gains in worker productivity, reduced absenteeism at work and school, and enhanced quality of life."

Like a car, our bodies need to be maintained, or we may need new parts or not make it. Programs already exist, showing the benefits of getting people up and moving and choosing better foods. They need to be encouraged and have accountability. Jenny Craig emphasizes eating more fruits and vegetables high in fiber and reducing junk food (processed sugars and fats). Food prescriptions in Indiana and Pennsylvania have shown significant improvements in weight loss and blood sugar levels in patients with type-2 diabetes (HgA1C -average blood sugars— dropping from

9.6 to 7.5).[48] Health is a choice but can be challenging in our day and age. What do you see when you drive down your main streets? In our town of Tampa, burger joints far outnumber places to get wholesome fruits and vegetables. The great part is, it's the people who decide who gets business or not.

Pledging your allegiance to the establishments that improve your health (rather than wreck it) can bring you and your family great rewards. Take your health back now. It's a lot more challenging if you continue to wait. Health is a gift, often taken for granted until it goes away!

Motivation

People like to win. Friendly competitions motivate folks. This is why shows like 'CrossFit' or 'The Biggest Loser' have become so popular. The goal is to get people stronger and build up their immune system, rather than wait for illness to take hold. Sure, people may still get sick, but with the armor of good nutrition, stronger muscles, bones, and

---

[48]Gralnick, Meg Tirrell, Jodi. 2018. "Diabetes Defeated by Diet: How New Fresh-Food Prescriptions Are Beating Pricey Drugs." *CNBC*. Retrieved from https://www.cnbc.com/2018/06/20/diabetes-defeated-by-diet-new-fresh-food-prescriptions-beat-drugs.html

mental well-being, they usually can overcome a lot quicker or may become more resilient to illness.

Coming back to the Land

Fortunately, we are seeing a shift to the good ole days where people (including many younger adults) are taking it upon themselves to grow their own fruits and vegetables. More local gardens are popping up in communities, schools, and personal homes. Some even have indoor gardens that seem fool-proof (i.e., vertical garden, aero garden).

My husband and I have two black thumbs, but following the instructions for the aero garden, we have been able to grow delicious herbs and lettuces from a platform half the size of a microwave. We also recently purchased a vertical outdoor hydroponic garden, but the results are not in yet. ☺

There are compost kits that you can easily buy or make one yourself that don't smell. In inner cities, where fresh fruits and vegetables can be hard to come by (not only in finding them but in price), these community gardens can offer residents an affordable alternative. It unites folks, getting them to work outside together, and it's rewarding to eat something you have grown. It's a great solution to a national obesity epidemic, where most people's food sources are fast food. There is a program in Chicago that buses in fresh fruits and vegetables to indigent areas that otherwise would be lacking.[49] According to former President Obama, there are some areas in Chicago where it's easier to purchase a gun than fresh vegetables.[50] That's tragic.

Taste

If you have ever picked your own fruit or vegetables, you should agree that they taste and look different from what you find in a supermarket; typically sweeter, and varying in size. Mass produced fruits and veggies are usually the same size because they have been cloned. They also have diminished taste from years ago…frequently even lacking any smell. Have you ever noticed that even flowers in the store don't always have a smell to them?

Excess sugar and salt can also numb your taste buds, to

---

[49] Lisa Waterman Gray, 2019. "Fresh Produce Deliveries Improve Nutrition in Chicago." *Food Tank*. Retrieved from https://foodtank.com/news/2019/09/mobile-markets-improve-fresh-produce-access-in-chicago-neighborhoods/

[50] DNAinfo Staff. " "Obama: It's Easier to Get a Gun Than Vegetables in Parts of Chicago." *DNAinfo Chicago*. Retrieved from https://www.dnainfo.com/chicago/20151027/south-loop/obama-its-easier-get-gun-than-vegetables-parts-of-chicago/

the point where you don't even realize how sweet or salty something already is. Imagine eating an orange after eating a regular chocolate bar. It may be the sweetest orange, but may now taste bitter to you because your taste buds have been reconditioned. That may explain why I have seen a medical assistant add sugar and whipped cream to her watermelon, and others add salt to an already salty soup. Good news — you can go back to the way our Creator intended whole foods to work for our bodies. If you begin limiting your sugar intake (which is one of the best ways to reduce weight and get healthy), you can taste real sweetness again!

Changing Legislation

In California, they found many fast-food chains target lower-income neighborhoods (providing them with cheap food). However, now, the legislation is intervening to limit how many fast-food restaurants can be in certain areas.

I think this push should continue. Currently, the Department of Agriculture subsidizes corn and soybean crops, which produce high fructose corn syrup and soybean oil, both of which are very unhealthy. These items are placed in many fast food items. Fortunately, consumers and other health advocates are speaking out against this tragedy, and I see fewer foods with these items. Wouldn't it make more sense to subsidize organic fruits and vegetables or hand them out to patients as food prescriptions? You may think I jest, but as I mentioned earlier, this is going on today at the Geisinger Institute in Philadelphia. As the results have been promising among diabetic patients, sister offices are opening in Indiana and at my alma mater UNC, Chapel Hill.

Better Marketing

Billions are spent on advertising, including specific ads targeting children. From the time they are young to adulthood, American children will see thousands of commercials for fast food, which can fatten them, making them prone to diabetes, heart disease, and cancer. Can you even count on one hand, how many advertisements you have seen for fresh fruits and vegetables?

Of note, many countries outside of the US have **banned** harmful food marketing to kids.

The NEW COOL

What if we changed the culture and began educating our kids about proper nutrition and staying active, using role models as spokespeople? There could be billboards of actors displaying healthy habits! What if we showed Oprah riding a bike, a commercial of Usher drinking a green juice or enjoying a fruit popsicle or smoothie, and Dwane Johnson "The Rock" eating a salad? What if we made it **NORMAL** and **COOL** to **LIVE WELL** and strange NOT to? Seriously, we call people who care about their health NUTS, but who really is? I've been labeled a "health nut" because I exercise and eat healthy. I feel great as a result and rarely get sick.

Many Americans are like this guy, a couch potato whose staple diet is junk food (SAD). They DON'T feel good. They suffer from obesity, heart disease, diabetes, high cholesterol, and arthritis. Seriously, who's NUTS?

Have you asked your doctor about…?

Of note, the US and New Zealand are the only two countries where direct to consumer (DTC) advertising for prescription drugs is still legal. Patients tell me they would rather deal with the disease, than all the harmful side effects.

Change Conditioning

I get why people buy fast food because it tastes good, it's convenient, it can cost less, and they are conditioned to. But as people were trained to eat poorly, they can be trained to eat better. Looking at the good ole days, people ate REAL FOOD because that's all there was. If you educate folks to eat SMART FOOD (helping them to understand eating is for nutrition, but it can also taste good, and be affordable) and teach them what's really in junk food, (often loaded with processed sugar, unhealthy fats and protein, including many chemicals, and hormones, with little nutrients), you can create NEW conditioning.

Interestingly, in Jerusalem*, while we saw many restaurants packed, this was the first time I saw a McDonald's empty...McDonald's is fairly new to Israel, and no one has been conditioned to eat there.

*The typical Israeli diet is Mediterranean, packed with many fresh, delicious tasting vegetables and legumes, i.e. hummus, which McDonald's lacks.

Prevention & Staying Well

Preventing illness is nothing new. Before meds, people had to rely on themselves, and there were healers knowledgeable about botanical remedies and what we needed to stay strong.

Self-care is not a new concept. For most of us, we practiced this since birth. As babies, we slept when we were tired and cried when we needed something. We ate when we were hungry and stopped when we were full. Our bodies could stretch like a doll where we sucked our toes and laughed unconditionally, cooing, and gurgling to communicate and be playful. We actively explored our world with curiosity and wonder and felt innate happiness. We enjoyed life for just being present. The nice part of this is that all we have to do is remember. The gifts are still there.

But what happened?

We grew up. Responsibilities hit, and our bodies may have stiffened in the process. We might have forgotten that we used to laugh for no reason and wanted to play all the time. Growing up doesn't mean we have to lose all that. Being an adult doesn't have to be all about sacrifice, hardship, or being miserable — which may seem normal to some. It can include cultivating joy by focusing on it and adding playfulness and growth to the picture. Spice up your life— no need to remain serious all the time. Making progress on fun projects that are important to you can help you live a fulfilling life and add to your health.

Remember, your brain's design is to keep you alive by sticking you in the comfort zone, doing what you always did to get you what you always have, because it works (you're still here), but that will never really give you the exciting life you deserve. It can make life mundane (knowing what to expect without much variety). While that may be fine for some, many individuals crave additional diversity to enhance their life.

Focus on the Solution

Focusing on the problems in the healthcare system is not going to fix it. Instead, we need to focus on viable solutions. Blame will not solve anything. All of us need to work together and ask ourselves if the actions we take will serve our nation in boosting the health outcomes of its citizens.

Take Back Your Health

We, as a nation, need to take responsibility. Like your finances, who will care most about YOUR Health? Correct... YOU! Once we do this, we can see real change. Don't rely just on what others tell you, read up on it, and make sure it makes sense for you!

That's why a grassroots action plan can help (as it did with removing BPA from baby bottles) along with some legislative policies that are more health-promoting (focusing on prevention and wellness). For example, making it easier to find affordable nutritious food options. Food prescriptions are a great way to begin, along with subsidizing or allowing folks to deduct fruit and vegetable purchases from their taxes. This can be compensated in part by taxing processed sugar. As people get healthier, we would see even more profits (as there would be less health expenditures). To boost local economies a large portion of these food items could come from local farmers.

It's a Start

Who would have thought McDonalds would offer salads, apples, and veggie burgers, or that Chick-Fil-A and Panda

Express would offer kale and broccoli. Panda Express also has brown rice? Of course, there is room for growth, but that's progress. I am still waiting to hear back from McDonald's corporation for my suggestion of offering whole grain buns.

DISCLAIMER BEFORE BEGINNING ANY EXERCISE PROGRAM PLEASE CHECK WITH YOUR DOCTOR!

FUN Moves

"If it's FUN, it'll get done!" **-Richard Simmons, Fitness Guru & Emmy award-winning talk show host for "The Richard Simons Show"**

With so much talk about obesity and health, as I mention in Habit #2, ACTION is the only real game changer. I've had many patients who tell me they're so tired. Increasing activity gives you more oomph by increasing blood flow and raising endorphins. Let's practice now!

FUN Moves

First, take 3 deep breaths and smile.

Take a moment to think of any activities you love to do (or what you can tolerate!)

Now, take 5 minutes to write them all down.

Again, don't hold back.

Look at your list.

What have you come up with? Schedule it. Make the time to do it!

Also think about if you like activities with others, alone and/or with a trainer.

Do you like to GLOW or if you are just getting started or recovering from an injury, a gentler activity i.e. Tai chi, chair/pool exercises, biking, and stretching may be more suitable.

The mind is powerful. You can simulate any activity, just move your body. Smiling and laughing help! As we spoke about earlier, you MAKE TIME for what's important. Fit it in and set it as a priority (because your health is!). I have patients who train before work, during lunch, after work, or while they are working. Do it when you can. For those who are just getting started, it's momentum. One trick my patient learned is to put his gym bag in the car (otherwise, he found himself on the couch watching TV). Personally, I dress in activewear clothing suitable for the office. That way I can exercise right after I'm done seeing patients — sometimes in the parking lot if need be…and I have less laundry! ☺

The main thing is that you do something and not sit on your duff. I never met anyone who regretted this. It keeps you young, energized, and strengthens your immune system. We all need this especially during this chaotic period in history, and now with more people home, they have the time to do this. I know of no pill that comes even close to all the benefits that activity offers. What works for you, and if it's not happening, get help? For some, they do need a trainer to get themselves motivated and make sure they exercise properly, don't over-train, and have fun. Find a good match for you.

Quick Workouts

High Intensity Interval Training (HIIT) are short workouts. They increase metabolism and burn more calories.

There's even a fitness group called "20 minutes to fitness" in Tampa, that claims 20 minutes a week is all it takes to get healthy. The American Heart Association guidelines recommend 30 minutes 5 times a week plus resistance training, but I would rather you do something than nothing at all.[51] If this gets you stronger and motivated, so be it and remember to have FUN in the process.

Some tips for fitness

- Park far away

- Take the stairs

- Dance while you clean

---

[51]"American Heart Association Recommendations for Physical Activity in Adults." Retrieved from https://atgprod.heart.org/HEARTORG/HealthyLiving/PhysicalActivity/StartWalking/American-Heart-Association-Recommendations-for-Physical-Activity-in-Adults_UCM_307976_Article.jsp

- Stretch while you are in line.

- Doctor's appointments— I rarely sit while I am waiting— usually, I'm stretching, doing heel lifts, and in the room, I do pushups and burpees. (Get it in while you can.)

- Standing desk (prolonged sitting, without activity, has shown to increase mortality)[52]

- Peddling (using the Peddler $30) while typing away or a treadmill while completing paperwork[53] [54]

Misconceptions dispelled

1. I need dairy to strengthen my bones.

The countries with the highest dairy consumption also showed the highest rates of osteoporosis.[55] You need

---

[52]"Sitting Time Linked to Higher Risk of Death from All Causes." Retrieved from https://www.cancer.org/latest-news/sitting-time-linked-to-higher-risk-of-death-from-all-causes.html

[53]"Peddler Working out at Work $30 - Google Search." Retrieved from https://www.google.com/search?rlz=1C1CHFX_enUS815US815&q=peddler+working+out+at+work+$30&tbm=isch&source=univ&sa=X&ved=2ahUKEwiZ1qu6yMTnAhVYop4KHeCyCswQsAR6BAgFEAE&biw=1280&bih=588&dpr=2

[54]"Treadmill at Work - Google Search." Retrieved from https://www.google.com/search?q=treadmill+at+work&rlz=1C1CHFX_enUS815US815&oq=treadmill+at+work&aqs=chrome..69i57.4754j0j9&sourceid=chrome&ie=UTF-8

[55] 2018. "Osteoporosis Linked to Drinking Milk - Latest Scientific Research." *IPhysio*. Retrieved from https://iphysio.io/osteoporosis/

calcium with vitamin D3, vitamin K2, phosphorous, and magnesium, among other things, to build strong bones along with weight-bearing exercises and good hormonal balance. Adequate calcium can come from dark green vegetables, sardines and salmon, and vitamin D3 from fish oil or supplements. K2 is found in fermented food and phosphorous and magnesium in nuts and seeds, and seafood. The concern is about conventional dairy and how the animals are treated. They are usually cramped in tight quarters, given growth hormones, and treated inhumanely. I get my goat's milk from a local farmer[56]. The animals are able to roam freely (you can meet them if you like), and the milk is not pasteurized.

2. Alcohol & caffeine are good for me

These are not nutrients. Alcohol is considered a toxin, and no medical guidelines recommend starting a drinking program if you don't already do so. Amount matters and too much can be harmful and lead to side effects and addiction. Typically for alcohol, one drink a day for women and two

---

[56] "The Dancing Goat - Home | Facebook." Retrieved from
https://www.facebook.com/dancinggoatdairy/

drinks a day for men (1oz liquor, 5oz glass of wine, or a 12 oz can of beer). However, it does increase the risk of breast cancer, even one drink a day.[57]

Caffeine: 1-2 *normal* cups of coffee a day should be okay if there are no sleep problems, anxiety, reflux, digestive issues, palpitations, etc. If you develop difficulties, you can simply switch to a healthy substitution, or if you don't want to wait to develop them, you can start these alternatives now. For alcohol, there are non-alcoholic beverages, i.e., black beer, ginger beer. For coffee, I suggest **low acid organic** and there is Teecino (coffee flavored tea).

3. Can I eat meat and eggs?

Some studies show if it's 100% grass-fed or pasture-raised in smaller amounts should be fine (where the animals are not given hormones or antibiotics, unless they're sick). The livestock that are grain-fed tend to be more inflammatory. In general, I like to source mine locally, where I can visit the farm. Eating eggs won't usually raise cholesterol by much. It is saturated fat that does that.[58]

---

[57] "Drinking Alcohol." *Breastcancer.Org*. Retrieved from
https://www.breastcancer.org/risk/factors/alcoho
[58] Kris Gunnars, BSc, 2018. "Eggs and Cholesterol — How Many Eggs Can You Safely Eat?" *Healthline*. Retrieved from

4. Are all fats bad?

Here are some facts on the "Good Fats" & more: [59] [60] [61] [62] [63]

A. Can reduce the risk of heart attacks & strokes (unlike bad fats which raise your risk)

B. Promotes normal brain (& nervous system) function

C. Absorbs nutrients (i.e. vitamin D) & stores energy

D. Precursor to making hormones, including estrogen, progesterone & testosterone and vitamin D (also a hormone).

E. Anti-inflammatory (good for arthritis)

F. Good Fats: omega 3 fatty acids i.e. fish oil (freeze caps), avocados, nuts & seeds

---

https://www.healthline.com/nutrition/how-many-eggs-should-you-eat

[59] Publishing, Harvard Health. n.d. "Getting to the Heart of the Fat Issue." *Harvard Health*. Retrieved from https://www.health.harvard.edu/mens-health/getting-to-the-heart-of-the-fat-issue

[60] Honor Whiteman, 2014. "A Diet Low in Saturated Fat 'Will Not Prevent Heart Disease or Prolong Life.'" Retrieved from (https://www.medicalnewstoday.com/articles/273528).

[61] Kathleen Doheny "Saturated Fats: Bad, Not Bad?" Retrieved from https://www.webmd.com/heart-disease/news/20140320/dietary-fats-q-a#1

[62]"Know Your Risk for Heart Disease | Cdc.Gov." Retrieved from (https://www.cdc.gov/heartdisease/risk_factors.htm).

[63]"Dietary Fats: Know Which Types to Choose - Mayo Clinic." Retrieved from (https://www.mayoclinic.org/healthy-lifestyle/nutrition-and-healthy-eating/in-depth/fat/art-20045550).

G. Bad Fats (e.g. damaged fats): trans fats[64]

H. More studies are questioning whether all saturated fats are bad for you. I personally like oils high in medium chain triglycerides (MCTs) and cook with coconut oil and Kerrygold butter.

Growing up, I was taught "fat is bad" and that eating "low fat foods" is healthier. Before this craze, a famous research investigation called "The Seven Countries Study" by Ancel Keys supported an association between saturated fat and an increased risk of heart disease. Some recent studies, however, have not shown such an association. Moreover, the actual low-fat foods that most Americans ate contained added sugar to improve the taste. Sadly, rates of heart disease, diabetes, and obesity skyrocketed. Of course, there were other factors involved, but consuming more processed sugar certainly contributed.

Ironically now the trend is "fat is good," with many people adopting higher fat diets (paleo, keto, or modified versions) with intermittent fasting. While there is merit to this, and many of my patients have found benefit, I still offer

---

[64]"Dietary Fats." *Www.Heart.Org.* Retrieved from
https://www.heart.org/en/healthy-living/healthy-eating/eat-smart/fats/dietary-fats

some words of caution. I don't believe there is ONE WAY to eat for everyone, and just because a food is healthy, doesn't mean it's healthy for you. Tweak and monitor and find out what your body needs. This can be tested through a nutritional and gut evaluation, which Dr. Gold can help you with if you're interested.

***

Further Food for Thought

"Let food be thy medicine" Hippocrates

At the doctor's offices, food prescriptions could be doled out more often than written prescriptions. Kids and their families could be given bags of fruits and vegetables, along with recipes. Classes in nutrition, reading labels, and how to cook and prepare tasty, healthy, quick and affordable meals, could be offered early in a child's education, and throughout life. This can be reiterated at office visits and special classes.

As families learn what's in processed foods and in the chemical scents that they breathe (including colognes, perfumes, deodorants, scented candles, plug-ins, and sprays), they'll be more apt to using more natural products that are plant-based. This information is paramount to lasting health, and much more useful than what I learned in my home economics class in the 1980s, of how to bake a chocolate cake from a Betty Crocker box.

So, where does laughter fit in?

"It's hard to be sad when you're happy" **-Wayne Dyer**

You can use it as a complementary modality for almost any condition. I have had patients who are laughing more, who no longer need certain medications (myself and my husband included).

We see many folks display sour emotions (albeit anger, frustration, sadness, or fear), which can be remedied with laughter. Even if it's contrived, it can cause the body to release endorphins, helping one feel better by releasing natural pain killers. So the notion of faking it until you make it or "acting happy" can trick the brain to feeling these emotions, and thereby gathering its benefits.

A novel approach

"I'm sorry," the nurse forewarned me, "she's a difficult patient, and there's nothing that can be done. Don't feel bad." Growing up in New York, I was up for the challenge!

As I entered the room, a petite Frenchwoman with emerald green eyes and short red hair, sat sobbing loudly in front of me. In the corner was her husband, a stout Asian man, his arms crossed, glaring at me. She had a long list of all the medications she tried and specialists she had seen, that didn't help her. I knew I needed a new strategy. Discussing only her grim prognosis would reinforce what she already knew, and would not break her state. She had been diagnosed with major depressive disorder for over 20 years. I wanted her to feel better NOW. My first question after introductions took her by surprise, "what makes you happy?"

Stunned, she just stared at me, and I repeated the question. "Sorry, no doctor has *ever* asked me that question before." After more silence, she replied with a smile, "the chicken dance. "Huh?" She reminisced of her first date with her husband.

I saw his arms relax down, and as she began to smile, so did he. Frances spoke of meeting him at a military formal in Hawaii. He showed her how to do this silly dance, and soon thereafter, they fell madly in love. I asked her to show me what that looked like. Reluctant at first, she finally agreed with the caveat "only if my husband joins me." "No way," he shook his head adamantly, but I countered with, "come on, if it's for your wife's health." She seemed to coax him too with her puppy dog eyes, and he finally relented.

At first hesitant to even begin, I encouraged them both and said I would follow their lead. Once relaxed, all of us got into a rhythm with our arms flapping and began to crack ourselves up. She told me she couldn't remember the last time she laughed or even smiled. Her husband agreed. The nurse knocked on the door to make sure everything was OK. After laughing so hard, it was challenging to stop. I still needed to listen to Frances' heart and lungs.

Once the physical exam was over, they resumed the chicken dance. It felt so good!

Like two teenagers, they danced into the lobby and continued their guffaws, oblivious to the stares.

She and her husband thanked me and the front desk for the "most effective, yet *unusual* doctor's visit they have ever had."

After they left, the nurses rushed up to me and asked me what the heck happened in there. She *laughed it off*! **It's difficult to be SAD when you're GLAD! And NO NEED**

to be WEARY when you're CHEERY!

What's Love got to do with it!

I would be remiss if I didn't speak about passion, intimacy, and sensuality as it pertains to happiness. As Dr. Ruth's sentiments would probably echo, it's important, and we're never too old to get some! All of us need to feel connected— to know we are loved and supported.

For those of you who may not know this incredible woman, Dr. Ruth is a sex therapist who gained notoriety on her radio talk show "Sexually Speaking," (1980-1990)…She is probably best recognized for talking frankly about sex in her cute thick German accent. With her petite frame and radiant smile, she is a bundle of energy. She's still kickin' in her 90's and her documentary "Ask Dr. Ruth" has just been released. In my opinion, she is the epitome of living with zest and is definitely another of my role models.

How love is defined can vary for each person. For some, it's engaging in a healthy sexual relationship. For others, it's retaining close intimacy through touch— hugs, massages, soft kisses, caressing someone else. People may even find pleasure in discovering their own bodies. There are many ways, but it's important not to discount this important means of bringing more smiles and genuine love into your life. People who have been married or together for many moons and are still deeply passionate in their relationships (yes, these people exist, and I've been fortunate to meet some of them) can give the rest of the world some pointers on how to keep the love alive. One thing I was taught is not to take the other person for granted and mix it up! Notice that I use the word healthy as there are unhealthy relationships that can lead to obsession or rumination about the other person or engaging in unsafe practices. YOU COME FIRST and make sure to take care of yourself. It's ok to think of the long-term effects and not just the moment. They say one can get caught up, and that's true, but it's important to be vigilant.

Sex, in a mutual, mature, loving relationship can be quite beautiful. It's also healthy for you. One study shows men who engage in intercourse at least twice a week can reduce their risk of heart disease by half. If the drive is gone, get a workup (especially with an integrative physician) and check your hormones. This natural act can make you more resilient to getting sick and help challenges seem more bearable (likely from lowering your cortisol levels and raising your endorphins). Even pain can lessen improving menstrual cramps.[65] Instead of Midol ladies, go for that Big O. Anxiety seems to melt away while the heart quickens in an exciting way when your loved one is around. You may get lost in each other's gaze and smile without knowing why. I am a hopeless romantic and there are tons of references in the media on this topic. Just look at covers of magazines (how to know if he's into you), romantic songs (think of the Beatles "All you need is Love") or the romantic movie channels or passionate, heated love novels. One of my favorites to read as a young girl was *Clan of the Cave Bears*.

If life has gotten boring in the bedroom, know it may need to heat up in the kitchen, maybe even over the sink! ☺ It's good to spice it up and HAVE FUN. Don't be afraid to PLAY and be Silly. Enjoy a long foreplay and become familiar with each other all over again. Do different things! Send love notes (people rarely do that nowadays, and it can be as simple as finding a love poem) and adding a rose, not just on Valentine's Day. There are many experts who can help in this arena, and it's important. I do believe in therapy

---

[65]"5 Common Questions About Sex and Your Heart – Health Essentials from Cleveland Clinic." Retrieved from https://health.clevelandclinic.org/why-sex-is-good-for-your-health-especially-your-heart

and counseling, not just when things are going wrong but to prevent them from happening. The "Naked Marriage" podcast has been an invaluable source for tips on how to continue to *date* your spouse. Your mate doesn't come with a manual, so you must learn from one other, working to meet each other's needs. It's not easy, far from it, but so worth it. Guidance helps. We all make mistakes, but finding forgiveness and being true to yourself, can set you *FREE*.

Think of the last time when you've truly been in love— crazy in love - that you couldn't stop thinking of the other person, and they felt the same way. How did that make you feel? You probably couldn't stop smiling or giggling. If you haven't felt this way in a while, know there's still a spark inside of you ready to ignite.

It's still there and can light you up in an instant. It's powerful. Even as babies, we need to be nurtured. Babies who are held and cuddled thrive, compared to those that aren't. In stark contrast, isolation is a form of torture. Think of what they do to prison inmates.

That's why, as we get older, it's so critical that we continue to connect, get outside, mingle, and interact with others, forming strong friendships and loving relationships.

Doing the things that matter!

In the wake of COVID-19 now more than ever, we need to bond with one another (even while practicing physical distancing).

As I write this, my niece graduated from nursery school on Zoom today. Do you know what most of the kids said they would miss and cherish the most? No, not the toys, but **their friends.**

Well folks since you began reading this book, I feel we are kindred spirits and yes friends (who I consider part of my loving family). I feel so honored to share a part of me with you. I do hope you enjoyed our journey together and will pass this along to your friends. As you progress in life, I encourage you to look at this book again with NEW EYES.

Remember you're *never* too old to FLOURISH, BE ACTIVE and HAVE FUN. In fact, your health and happiness depend on it! **Dr.'s Orders!** ☺

Truopia: The Future

Imagine a place where people live long, fulfilling lives. They die of old age, rather than from heart disease, cancer, stroke, or medical errors. They take few pills if any, and rely on natural remedies, including healthy eating, exercise, and their sense of humor. Things don't always go as planned, but they focus on what they can do about it and let things go.

The local hospital has to close down its doors because there aren't enough sick people. Instead, they are turning it into a wellness center, with a large heated pool, adult playground (where kids can play too with jungle gyms, trampolines, and swings) and state of the art kitchens for cooking and nutrition classes. They will also offer dance and laughter classes, gymnastics, basketball, pickleball, hockey and soccer, among many other activities for all age groups including seniors.

Best of all, Medicare and other insurances will cover this! The fast-food restaurants are about to shut their doors, not enough customers. People don't want processed food anymore. The owners caring about their customer's welfare willingly change their menus. These fast food establishments, now known as "Savvy Food" gastronomics, begin offering REAL FOOD (from the earth) that tastes good, is affordable, and is good for your body, now known as SMART FOOD!! Goodbye Big Mac, hello McSmoothie.

People feel better and thrive, rather than merely survive! This place I speak of, I call Truopia (the true world). Our bodies have an innate ability to function well and heal when given the right circumstances.

It may seem farfetched to think that most Americans will choose healthier lifestyles, but so did the concept of airplanes, rockets, and the world being round at one point in time. "It's the crazy ones who believe they can change the world that actually do!" Steve Jobs.

Further testament to this, is that it's already occurring. A group who called themselves the Black Hebrews settled in Israel and did just that. They recognized the Wealth of Health!

The Black Hebrews

This group of African Americans living in Chicago decided to follow the Old Testament and live as if they were in the Garden of Eden -eating REAL FOOD off the land. What better place than the Biblical land flowing with milk and honey- Israel. Much of the group grew up in a big city living on fast food and rarely moved. They were overweight, obese, battling a host of medical conditions, including diabetes, high blood pressure, high cholesterol and lots of stress. Suddenly they found themselves living on acres of sandy desolate land, having no actual skills in farming. No fret. They got busy and got to work. They set up their village and with all the medical problems opened a clinic. After a few years it was shut down.

Why? What happened?

The Black Hebrews got healthy. They began exercising regularly. They worked the land: planting crops and trees, building their own homes, and built up their town.

Until their crops came in, their neighbors, who were also farmers, shared their produce with them. Growing fruits and vegetables in a desert are miracles by themselves. It's incredible to taste a juicy red tomato that was just covered in sand - salty, delicious and so fresh!

The mounds of city life stress diminished as they felt part of something larger than themselves. Here in Dimona, they were creating a self-sustaining village. They were on a mission, determined, loving and working together.

The View

Their front and back yard could look out for miles and see beautiful landscapes instead of skyscrapers. The clean air rejuvenating their bodies, and allowed them to see vast blue skies free of major pollution. Cool and crisp air in the evening made it delightful after a hard day's work outside. Void of city streetlights and smog, the evenings depicted a breathtaking starry night, almost as seen through a telescope.

People back home thought they were crazy. Why would you leave a great paying job for this?

The benefits

As they consumed more wholesome delights and moved more, the pounds melted away. They trimmed down, (no need for Jenny Craig or Weight Watchers here). They were doing what their bodies were meant to do MOVE (Play, Sing and Dance.) Have FUN and live life fully. Their reward-

Good Health. Because the women (and men) got so healthy, (and fertile) and they had virtually no sick visits, they converted the clinic to a wellness center. It also doubled as a maternity ward and nursery.

My sister and I were fortunate to visit this place (considered a must see in our guidebooks). We witnessed their evening entertainment of enlivened singing and dancing and the strong bonds they formed. It reminded me of what went on in the old days when groups of Jews came to build the Kibbutzim (collective farms). It was hard work, but they rejoiced with singing and dancing as the Black Hebrews did so well that night.

A stark contrast of their former life where they spent the evenings in front of a TV wolfing down a pizza.

One man I'll call Joseph told me how when he first came here, he could barely move. His hands hurt and he suffered with disabling arthritis. After several months of eating better, exercising and laughing more (and just being outside), he feels incredible. He shed his muffin top and now loves going for a run through the fields.

Ask yourself, what makes more sense- to live well, or be ill on a pill? Of course, I am not saying to not take your medicines but WHY NOT work to get off them!

Improved Health

We can all improve our health and journey to Truopia. It's available to us, through the decisions we make every moment. Who will care more about YOUR health than YOU? YOU DESERVE TO FEEL BETTER!

Don't ever underestimate your power

Walking on the beach today, I stepped on a thorn. It hurt! Tiny, but mighty, I realized if something so little can have an impact, so can you. Remember even the smallest steps can create big results over time. Just think of the 'butterfly effect' and the law of compounding. It's the same with your wellness plan.

Decide and do something daily. This builds momentum and every decision (or lack thereof) has consequences. It can mean the difference between living your dream life or knowing it will never come to pass because you did nothing about it! YOU ARE POWERFUL, MIGHTY and STRONG.

I Believe in YOU! ♡ Believe in Yourself. Get to work, TAKE ACTION and get started NOW!

The means to a Joyful Life is YOU.

Dr. Tanya Gold, MD, is a board-certified family medicine and holistic medical doctor. She's also a certified yoga instructor and laughter yoga leader. Utilizing natural approaches to wellness, Dr. Gold believes in treating the whole person, including the root cause of an illness, and getting people to feel incredible.

At her medical office, Dr. Gold's Optimal Living Institute (aka D'goli) she takes the time needed to spend with patients, *to listen and hear their stories with compassion.* As part of her comprehensive workup, she orders specialized tests to evaluate their nutritional status, gut integrity, and hormone levels. In addition to routine labs, Dr. Gold also screens for toxins, allergies, and early heart disease markers. It's rewarding to wean patients off their prescriptions and have them improve long term... She loves working to *prevent* illness, rather than *wait* for it.

Dr. Gold understands that occasionally, patients need some handholding or a hug (or a modified version during COVID-19). That's why she'll do what it takes. Assisting them with workouts, shopping, cooking, and preparing healthy meals, along with showing them therapeutic stretches and how to laugh on purpose, are just some examples. She helps folks ignite the fire within so they can *LIVE OPTIMALLY!* ☺

Dr. Gold resides in Tampa FL with her husband and two misunderstood kitties.

Check out these sites to stay up to date on her latest events.

www.dgoli.com Dr. Gold's Optimal Living Institute	**Facebook** Dr. Gold's Optimal Living Institute
YouTube Dr. Gold Fun Yoga	**Twitter** Dr. Tanya Gold
Instagram	**LinkedIn** Dr. Tanya Gold

Bibliography

1. Marcus, Marina, M. Taghi Yasamy, Mark van van Ommeren, Dan Chisholm, and Shekhar Saxena. 2012. "Depression: A Global Public Health Concern: (517532013-004)."

2. 2017. *Chimpanzees Playing & Laughing.* https://www.youtube.com/watch?v=ffnyOZGB-Tc

3. Khamsi, Roxanne. 2005. "Laughter Boosts Blood-Vessel Health." *Nature* news050307-4. doi: 10.1038/news050307-4.

4. JMot Behav. 2014;46(1):33-7.doi10.1080/00222895.2013.844091. Epub 2013 Nov 18.

5. "Humor Helps Your Heart? How?" Retrieved from (https://www.heart.org/HEARTORG/Conditions/More/MyHeartandStrokeNews/Humor-helps-your-heart-How_UCM_447039_Article.jsp).

6. "BBC News | HEALTH | Laughter 'Protects the Heart.'" Retrieved from (http://news.bbc.co.uk/2/hi/health/1024713.stm).

7. Bennett, Mary Payne, and Cecile Lengacher. 2009. "Humor and Laughter May Influence Health IV. Humor and Immune Function." *Evidence-Based Complementary and Alternative Medicine : ECAM* 6(2):159–64. doi: 10.1093/ecam/nem149.

8. Miller, Michael, and William F. Fry. 2009. "The Effect of Mirthful Laughter on the Human Cardiovascular System." *Medical Hypotheses* 73(5):636–39. doi: 10.1016/j.mehy.2009.02.044.

9. Bains, Gurinder Singh, Lee S. Berk, Noha Daher, Everett Lohman, Ernie Schwab, Jerrold Petrofsky, and Pooja Deshpande. 2014. "The Effect of Humor on Short-Term Memory in Older Adults: A New Component for Whole-Person Wellness." *Advances in Mind-Body Medicine* 28(2):16–24.

10. Savage, Brandon M., Heidi L. Lujan, Raghavendar R. Thipparthi, and Stephen E. DiCarlo. 2017. "Humor, Laughter, Learning, and Health! A Brief Review." *Advances in Physiology Education* 41(3):341–47. doi: 10.1152/advan.00030.2017.

11. "Stress Relief from Laughter? It's No Joke - Mayo Clinic." Retrieved October 20, 2020

(https://www.mayoclinic.org/healthy-lifestyle/stress-management/in-depth/stress-relief/art-20044456).

12. "Mayo Mindfulness: Laughter for Stress Relief Is No Joke." *Https://Newsnetwork.Mayoclinic.Org/*. Retrieved from (https://newsnetwork.mayoclinic.org/discussion/mayo-mindfulness-stress-relief-with-laughter-is-no-joke/).

13. Newman, Tim 2019. "Do Antidepressants Work Better than Placebo?" Retrieved from (https://www.medicalnewstoday.com/articles/325767).

14. *Data Colada*. Retrieved from (http://datacolada.org/wp-content/uploads/2014/03/Strack-et-al-1988-cartoons.pdf).

15. Carney DR, Cuddy AJ, Yap AJ. "Power Posing: Brief Nonverbal Displays Affect Neuroendocrine Levels and Risk Tolerance - PubMed." Retrieved from (https://pubmed.ncbi.nlm.nih.gov/20855902/).

16. "You Will Never Speak Bad Words Again after

Watching This! The Power of Words Are HUGE - YouTube." Retrieved from (https://www.youtube.com/watch?v=MKy-DmnBdvI&t=14s).

17. Kop, W. J., Synowski, S. J., Newell, M. E., Schmidt, L. A., Waldstein, S. R., & Fox, N. A. (2011). Autonomic nervous system reactivity to positive and negative mood induction: the role of acute psychological responses and frontal electrocortical activity. Biological psychology, 86(3), 230–238. Retrieved from (https://www.ncbi.nlm.nih.gov/pmc/articles/PMC3061260/).

18. Sifferlin, Alexandra. "Eating Healthy Is Cheaper than You Think | TIME.Com." Retrieved from (https://healthland.time.com/2013/12/05/eating-healthy-is-cheaper-than-you-think/).

19. Settembre, Jeanette. "How Prescribing Healthy Food Could Save Billions of Dollars in Health-Care Costs - MarketWatch." Retrieved from (https://www.marketwatch.com/story/how-prescribing-healthy-food-could-save-billions-of-

dollars-in-health-care-costs-2019-03-21).

20. Publishing, Harvard Health. n.d. "Preserve Your Muscle Mass." *Harvard Health*. Retrieved from (https://www.health.harvard.edu/staying-healthy/preserve-your-muscle-mass).

21. I also use the iceberg analogy earlier to explain the "extra" ordinary but doable work it takes to be happy (see illustration Chapter 1).

22. Mindvalley. 2020. "How To Get Your Focus Back And Stop Procrastinating - Nir Eyal." *The Mindvalley Podcast With Vishen Lakhiani | Listen Now*. Retrieved from (https://podcast.mindvalley.com/how-to-get-your-focus-back-and-stop-procrastinating-nir-eyal/).

23. Conradt, Stacy "Why Walt Disney Built a Theme Park on Swampland | Mental Floss." Retrieved from (https://www.mentalfloss.com/article/28174/why-walt-disney-built-theme-park-swampland).

24. Bohanes, Michal "Following Your Passion' Is Dead - Here's What To Replace It With." Retrieved from (https://www.forbes.com/sites/michalbohanes/2018/

07/05/following-your-passion-is-dead-heres-what-to-replace-it-with/#3244414f7f83).

25. Nick Skillicorn "The TRUE Story of Post-It Notes, and How They Almost Failed - Idea to Value." Retrieved from (https://www.ideatovalue.com/insp/nickskillicorn/2017/04/true-story-post-notes-almost-failed/).

26. Leonhardt, David "Life Expectancy Data - The New York Times." Retrieved from (https://www.nytimes.com/2006/09/27/business/27leonhardt_sidebar.html).

27. "Nearly 7 in 10 Americans Take Prescription Drugs, Mayo Clinic, Olmsted Medical Center Find." *Https://Newsnetwork.Mayoclinic.Org/*. Retrieved from (https://newsnetwork.mayoclinic.org/discussion/nearly-7-in-10-americans-take-prescription-drugs-mayo-clinic-olmsted-medical-center-find/).

28. Dima M. Qato, G. Caleb Alexander, Jenny S. Guadamuz and Stacy Tessler Lindau "Prescription Medication Use Among Children and Adolescents in the United States | American Academy of

Pediatrics." Retrieved from
(https://pediatrics.aappublications.org/content/142/3
/e20181042).

29. & 30. Friedland, Robert B. *Ph.D.*. "Selected Long-
Term Care Statistics | Family Caregiver Alliance."
Retrieved from (https://www.caregiver.org/selected-
long-term-care-statistics).

31. "Anxiety Disorders: Types, Causes, Symptoms &
Treatments." Retrieved from
(https://my.clevelandclinic.org/health/diseases/9536
-anxiety-disorders).

32. "Facts & Statistics | Anxiety and Depression
Association of America, ADAA." Retrieved from
(https://adaa.org/about-adaa/press-room/facts-
statistics).

33. "Overweight & Obesity Statistics | NIDDK."
*National Institute of Diabetes and Digestive and
Kidney Diseases*. Retrieved from
(https://www.niddk.nih.gov/health-
information/health-statistics/overweight-obesity).

34. "About Chronic Diseases | CDC." Retrieved from
(https://www.cdc.gov/chronicdisease/about/index.ht

m).

35. Friedland, Robert B., Ph.D. "Selected Long-Term Care Statistics | Family Caregiver Alliance." Retrieved from (https://www.caregiver.org/selected-long-term-care-statistics).

36. Tanne, Janice. 2006. "US Gets Mediocre Results despite High Spending on Health Care." *BMJ : British Medical Journal* 333(7570):672.

37. Harrison Cook "Among 11 Countries, US Ranks Last for Health Outcomes, Equity and Quality." Retrieved from (https://www.beckershospitalreview.com/quality/among-11-countries-us-ranks-last-for-health-outcomes-equity-and-quality.html).

38. Brett Molina. "More than 1 in 3 Americans Eat Fast Food in a given Day, CDC Finds." Retrieved from (https://www.usatoday.com/story/news/nation-now/2018/10/03/americans-eat-fast-food-daily-cdc-survey/1507702002/).

39. 2016. "CDC Press Releases." *CDC*. Retrieved from (https://www.cdc.gov/media/releases/2017/p1116-fruit-vegetable-consumption.html).

40. Dennis Thomps. "Many U.S. Children Go Days without Eating Any Vegetables, Survey Finds." Retrieved from (https://www.cbsnews.com/news/children-not-eating-vegetables-survey/).

41. President's Council on Sports, Fitness &. Nutrition. 2012. "Facts & Statistics." *HHS.Gov*. Retrieved from https://www.hhs.gov/fitness/resource-center/facts-and-statistics/index.html).

42. Christof Baron "• Establishments in the U.S. Fast Food Industry 2018 | Statista." Retrieved from (https://www.statista.com/statistics/196619/total-number-of-fast-food-restaurants-in-the-us-since-2002/).

43. "Population & Food: Facts and Trivia." Retrieved from (http://www.foodreference.com/html/f-population-trivia.html).

44. "The Evolution of American Agriculture — Jayson Lusk." Retrieved from (http://jaysonlusk.com/blog/2016/6/26/the-evolution-of-american-agriculture).

45. July 16, Updated, 2020. "1800-1990: Changes In Urban/Rural U.S. Population." *SeniorLiving.Org.* Retrieved from (https://www.seniorliving.org/history/1800-1990-changes-urbanrural-us-population/).

46. US EPA, OAR. 2015. "Progress Cleaning the Air and Improving People's Health." *US EPA.* Retrieved from(https://www.epa.gov/clean-air-act-overview/progress-cleaning-air-and-improving-peoples-health).

47. "Half A Century Of The Health Care Crisis (And Still Going Strong)." Retrieved from (/do/10.1377/hblog20180904.457305/full).

48. Gralnick, Meg Tirrell, Jodi. 2018. "Diabetes Defeated by Diet: How New Fresh-Food Prescriptions Are Beating Pricey Drugs." *CNBC.* Retrieved from (https://www.cnbc.com/2018/06/20/diabetes-defeated-by-diet-new-fresh-food-prescriptions-beat-drugs.html).

49. Lisa Waterman Gray, 2019. "Fresh Produce Deliveries Improve Nutrition in Chicago." *Food*

Tank. Retrieved from
(https://foodtank.com/news/2019/09/mobile-markets-improve-fresh-produce-access-in-chicago-neighborhoods/).

50. DNAinfo Staff. "Obama: It's Easier to Get a Gun Than Vegetables in Parts of Chicago." *DNAinfo Chicago*. Retrieved from (https://www.dnainfo.com/chicago/20151027/south-loop/obama-its-easier-get-gun-than-vegetables-parts-of-chicago).

51. "American Heart Association Recommendations for Physical Activity in Adults." Retrieved from (https://atgprod.heart.org/HEARTORG/HealthyLiving/PhysicalActivity/StartWalking/American-Heart-Association-Recommendations-for-Physical-Activity-in-Adults_UCM_307976_Article.jsp).

52. "Sitting Time Linked to Higher Risk of Death from All Causes." Retrieved from (https://www.cancer.org/latest-news/sitting-time-linked-to-higher-risk-of-death-from-all-causes.html).

53. "Peddler Working out at Work $30 - Google

Search." Retrieved from(https://www.google.com/search?rlz=1C1CHF X_enUS815US815&q=peddler+working+out+at+w ork+$30&tbm=isch&source=univ&sa=X&ved=2ah UKEwiZ1qu6yMTnAhVYop4KHeCyCswQsAR6B AgFEAE&biw=1280&bih=588&dpr=2).

54. "Treadmill at Work - Google Search." Retrieved from (https://www.google.com/search?q=treadmill+at+w ork&rlz=1C1CHFX_enUS815US815&oq=treadmil l+at+work&aqs=chrome..69i57.4754j0j9&sourceid =chrome&ie=UTF-8).

55. 2018. "Osteoporosis Linked to Drinking Milk - Latest Scientific Research." *IPhysio*. Retrieved from(https://iphysio.io/osteoporosis/).

56. "The Dancing Goat - Home | Facebook." Retrieved from (https://www.facebook.com/dancinggoatdairy/).

57. "Drinking Alcohol." *Breastcancer.Org*. Retrieved from (https://www.breastcancer.org/risk/factors/alcohol).

58. Kris Gunnars, BSc, 2018. "Eggs and Cholesterol —

How Many Eggs Can You Safely Eat?" *Healthline*. Retrieved from(https://www.healthline.com/nutrition/how-many-eggs-should-you-eat).

59. Publishing, Harvard Health. n.d. "Getting to the Heart of the Fat Issue." *Harvard Health*. Retrieved from (https://www.health.harvard.edu/mens-health/getting-to-the-heart-of-the-fat-issue).

60. Honor Whiteman, 2014. "A Diet Low in Saturated Fat 'Will Not Prevent Heart Disease or Prolong Life.'" Retrieved from (https://www.medicalnewstoday.com/articles/273528).

61. Kathleen Doheny "Saturated Fats: Bad, Not Bad?" Retrieved from (https://www.webmd.com/heart-disease/news/20140320/dietary-fats-q-a#1).

62. "Know Your Risk for Heart Disease | Cdc.Gov." Retrieved from (https://www.cdc.gov/heartdisease/risk_factors.htm)

63. "Dietary Fats: Know Which Types to Choose - Mayo Clinic." Retrieved from (https://www.mayoclinic.org/healthy-

lifestyle/nutrition-and-healthy-eating/in-depth/fat/art-20045550).

64. "Dietary Fats." *Www.Heart.Org*. Retrieved from (https://www.heart.org/en/healthy-living/healthy-eating/eat-smart/fats/dietary-fats).

65. "5 Common Questions About Sex and Your Heart – Health Essentials from Cleveland Clinic." Retrieved from (https://health.clevelandclinic.org/5-common-questions-about-sex-and-your-heart/).

CPSIA information can be obtained
at www.ICGtesting.com
Printed in the USA
LVHW081427170322
713445LV00002B/4